MOTION

MOTION

A JENTA STORY

BY

LENGDUNG TUNGCHAMMA

WALKING TOGETHER PRESS

ESTES PARK · JENTA MANGORO

Motion, A Jenta Story
© 2025 Lengdung Tungchamma

Walking Together Press
Estes Park, Colorado USA
Jenta Mangoro, Jos, Plateau Nigeria
walkingtogether.press

ISBN: 978-1-961568-71-6

Cover design and interior art by Jacoba Looije
Front cover portrait by Becky Awo Likita
Back cover photo by Andrew Sunnena

Typeset in Garamond Premier Pro by D. Thaine Norris

First Edition

Some names in this story have been changed for privacy.

ACKNOWLEDGMENTS

It was Thaine Norris who challenged me to write this book, yet I had many excuses against the project. First, I didn't know how to write a book. Second, a memoir at this stage of my life seemed too early. However, I was ultimately convinced when Thaine pointed out that this isn't my story alone; it is also the story of my community and how it is impacted by the Jenta Reads Community Library. It is a story of hope for future Jenta generations. Then, Thaine joined me in the writing adventure as an editor, proofreader, encourager, and guest writer. There are no words to describe my indebtedness. Thank you, Pops!

Many thanks to Erika Norris, Eb Roell, and Kevin Mote for their thoughtful feedback after reading the first draft. Special thanks to Helena Sorenson, whose editing pushed this book to the final stage.

Without my wife, Senfat Tungchamma, this book would have taken years. She made it easier with the conversations she fostered and encouraged. It was a blessing that we attended the same secondary school. Our conversations triggered memories and created an environment that allowed me to write about them. Thank you, Baby Girl.

I owe a debt to many friends and family members who have helped me along the way. You will meet some of them in this book.

I am indebted to my sisters for helping me search for family photos. Jacoba Looije, a God-send, designed the amazing book cover and interior art.

Many thanks to the fantastic team who made Jenta Reads possible. Jenta Reads is not my idea. It is the idea of a community of young men and women who believe God has a plan for them and their community. It is my blessing to be a part of this team. May God grant us more years and wisdom to continue this work that He has started in us and through us.

Soli Deo Gloria.

Lengdung Tungchamma
Jenta Mangoro
Jos, Nigeria

Contents

To Mother, who believed even before it was time.

*"The first generation thinks about survival;
the ones that follow tell the stories."*
—Hua Hsu, Stay True

I am the second generation, and it is time to tell the stories.

Ghetto Boy, Jenta Boy

*"An object will remain in a state of rest or uniform
motion unless an external force acts upon it."*

I was born in Jenta. My family had just moved into a new house they built with their own hands in early 1997. In May of that year, I arrived in this world. Mother wanted to name me "Lurit," meaning "new home." However, Father rejected it. He declared that the name would be "Lengdung," which means "thinks deeply" in Ngas. When broken down into two syllables, "Leng" and "dung," it would mean "spoiled soup." Life had two paths for me. Which would it be? "Lengdung" or "Leng dung?" I am still on the journey.

Rough Beginning

My father and mother had ten children—five boys and five girls. Four boys and one girl died in childhood, while four girls and one boy survived. I was that boy. Charity, Ritdirnen, Walkat, and Yilrit are the girls. My parents told me that I exhibited unusual frailty, and they feared I would not live to adulthood. Surprisingly, and by God's grace, I survived. They said I wasn't eating, that I was always falling ill, and they constantly took me to the hospital, more than any other child they had. I had a hole in the top of my head, which terrified them, leading to fears that I might develop cognitive impairments. In their minds, even if I survived, I might still become a burden.

My parents buried one child after another. Devastating is an understatement. There are no words to describe the experience of losing a child. Dreams and hopes are shattered. For a poor family like mine, children may be the only legacy and the only way to aspire to higher things. Because life was mainly daily survival, my parents would tell themselves, "The things I cannot do, my child will do. The things I could not achieve, the child will achieve." The first child died, then the second, third, fourth, and fifth—each a reminder that life was unfair and that those dreams were even further out of reach. It was an unbearable, constant fear for them. The universe itself seemed set against them. Each time Mother was pregnant, they were on edge—watching, wondering, struggling against that universe, trying to keep just this one. Losing so many children in the early years of their marriage scarred them for life.

Father

My parents were not rich. Even so, they were amongst the most comfortable in their community. You see, my parents are first-generation city dwellers. When my dad arrived in the city from a village in Kanke Local Government Area of Plateau State, he came with nothing. All he had was himself. He was not particularly religious, never has been. He had not completed his primary education when he moved to the city. According to him, his father never cared much about education. When a new school session started and his father didn't have money for school fees and uniform, that became the end of his "education".

More than anything else, the fact of his dropping out of school would determine the course of the rest of his life. By dropping out, it simply meant that his options were limited. The best job he would ever have was a cleaner. Whenever I think about this, one fact strikes me: if hard work were a person, he would certainly be my dad. My dad works so hard that it intimidates me. However, without a level of education to match his dedication, he would not reach his full potential despite all his hard work.

One of his favorite phrases is, "Hard work has never killed anyone. Can you show me anyone who has died of hard work?" Sometimes, I want to retort, "But hard work is not enough. Smart work is more important." I never have.

My dad defined his identity by his ability to provide food for us at home. To him, a real man provides for his family. There was one way he showed this very much. He brought gifts for us every evening when he returned from work. Back in the day, he would borrow from friends to ensure he brought something home. As the years of struggle became more difficult, he stopped bringing gifts home. Not having gifts ate him up, and the hurt began to show in his behavior when he came home. He would react negatively to anything. He would vent his pent-up anger at everyone or everything. Even then, I understood that he was not reacting to us. He was responding to his new station in life. He was angry at what life had done to him. Diminished. Stolen valor. It had made him less of a man. And nothing was more degrading for a man who loved to be a man.

The circumstances that led my father to obtain his government job should have been an indicator of the future travails he would face. As a child, I did not know the whole story, and even now, as an adult, I can only say that Nigeria confounds me.

This was the story I was told.

There lived an uncle within my mother's family, a reputable police officer who rose to the rank of Assistant Superintendent of Police in

The Nigerian Police Force. On one occasion, my father helped provide medication for one of his children. Out of an abundance of gratitude, he asked my parents to provide a person to whom he would give a job in the government. My parents asked about the job requirements, and he told them that any first-school leaving certificate holder could apply. It was the least educational qualification in Nigeria. Then they asked, why not my father? He had that qualification.

That's how he got the job as a constable, a lowly constable in charge of cleaning.

For a few years, Father was an office darling. He worked hard and earned preferential treatment. People respected him, but Father never let it go to his head. He arrived at work by 5 AM and left on time, never missing a day. And with a blood relative at the office, he received his promotions as they came up. There wasn't much trouble during those years.

But when my uncle retired and died a few years later, Father was all alone in an enormous bureaucracy that seemed intentionally hell-bent on crippling everyone. Being a dedicated staff member in Nigeria is divine, but getting promotions is human. Although Father served faithfully and never missed work, he never got his due promotions. Every time we got the opportunity to talk, he would rant about the promotions that never arrived.

This year, they told him the papers were before the state Commissioner of Police. Next year, they told him the papers were before the Inspector General of Police. Two years later, they told him the Inspector General of Police (IGP) had been replaced, so they had to restart all the processes from scratch. They would do the same thing all over again. The IGP is changed at least once every five years. Sometimes, he is forced to retire due to age. However, different priorities, loyalties, and dependents would force a change.

Such a system creates a dependency making millions of Nigerians depend on the average "Nigerian big man". The Nigerian big man is an influential, wealthy, and powerful person. An elite of the elite. The average Nigerian big man is expected to help his community before any other community. In a country like Nigeria, where a tribe is comprised of millions of people, it is not surprising that nepotism holds sway. Suppose you have to help your community before you help others. When would you finish assisting millions before you look to others? The painful reality is that if a public servant does not favor his people above others, he is considered a traitor and would never get any other public service role within that region. This favoritism is a suicide trap for altruistic men who want to rise in public service. Everything is attached to your "state of origin." If your state of origin considers you a traitor, you can forget a career in the public arena. No one will come to save you or defend you.

Of course, the consequence is that merit is sacrificed on the altar of nepotism. Hardworking individuals like my father never get what is due to them. My father languished for years, complained, prayed, and finally resigned to his fate. Seeing this injustice was the first thing that made me understand the nature of public service and sowed the seeds against government work in my heart. I knew then as I still do that I didn't want to spend my life in a system like this, fighting a war I could not win.

Throughout my teenage years, the one thing I prayed the hardest for was for my father to be promoted at work. It was only logical and just that my father, a dedicated worker, should rise through the ranks. Perhaps I thought that a promotion would lift us higher. As I think about it now, maybe it wouldn't have changed our fortunes much, but it would have provided a little more, allowing my father to take better care of us and himself. He didn't get any promotions. And we didn't get better care. Justice seemed like a logical thing to my teenage mind, but it turns out justice is an illogical thing to expect in Nigeria. This failed prayer request, the apparent need of my family in the eyes of a loving God was something I could not reconcile. Many other episodes will add to my dossier of cases against God.

Mother

In Jenta, we never call our parents "Mum" and "Dad." Those are words used by Ajebos, the children of the elites of Nigeria. Neither did we use pet names for our parents, they were far above that. Our culture of respect and honor demanded that we used a reverential term, one that showed our relationship with them. However, the reverence should not be too much. So we called our mum "Mumcy", and dad "Baba".

My father was not present in my childhood. Yes, he was there, but I was not conscious of him. My mother was everything. Mumcy ran the whole house. She was "Lord of the Manor." In a way, she was the man of the house. Baba made his presence known only when there were major decisions to make and when any of us children had committed a serious crime that deserved his punishment.

There are levels of punishment in Jenta.

Level One: The neighbor's punishment. This is the mildest punishment a child can get. In Jenta, anyone can punish any child who has committed an offense. As a child, I always prayed that if I did anything wrong, my neighbor would catch and punish me instead of taking me home.

Level Two: The mother's punishment. Mothers were not sparing when it came to punishment. They would beat you for the slightest reason. That was their love language. The mother's punishment is often more severe than that of the neighbor. Many times, you would even find the neighbor interceding for the child. But still, that is not the worst that could happen.

Level Three: The father's punishment. The father rarely beats the child, but it's like a wrestling match when he decides to. As a young adult, I enjoyed playing a PlayStation game called Mortal Kombat. After a fight, there's a stage called FINISH HIM. When fathers beat a child, it's the FINISH HIM stage. The beatings by fathers were rare but unforgettable. They would often leave you with a scar.

My father showed up when there was a need for the "finish him" stage. But in my case, it was not my father who left me with a scar. It was my mother. I like to think my mother was half lion, half human. She ran the household sternly. It was common in those days to have several cousins, aunties, and uncles in our house. One time, two of my uncles and an aunty stayed with us. Also, one of the uncles had just gotten married, so imagine running a house with twelve people in three rooms. I still don't know how she did that. She enforced order in all the ways possible. On this particular day, it was raining, and there was a clear command that no one should go out, but as you know, children always want to do the very thing they are told not to do. I wanted to go out into the rain and play.

A poor parent's greatest fear is for one of their wards to fall sick. Added to their poverty would be the burden of taking care of a sick person, which can be very expensive and time-consuming. My mother didn't want anyone out because she didn't want to have a sick child. Ignoring her instructions, I went out in the rain and played to my heart's content. When she realized I was outside, she invited me in as though she wanted to give me a gift. Foolishly, I went in. That day, she beat the demon out of me. While beating me, I tried to escape, but she was a strong woman, so it was a struggle. I fell and hit my nose on the edge of the solid, heavy wood bed frame. In a few seconds, blood was rushing out. Suddenly, that same woman who was beating me was the one trying to stop the bleeding—the contradictions of a mother.

She succeeded with the help of a local chemist in our community. However, the wound was permanent. It grew into a large boil that covered my mouth and eyes. Even after I completely healed, the scar remained. Whenever you meet me, there is a scar on my nose. It is the legacy of an African mother's discipline and love.

(My greatest regret about this episode was that it happened during the Christmas season. I couldn't eat any of those sweet things. Meat, chin chin, jollof rice, juice, and unique delicacies were only prepared on Christmas day. The wound on my face affected my ability to eat. Here's some advice for African mothers: don't beat your children close to Christmas; you will be disenfranchising them from their fundamental human right to enjoy a good Christmas season. Who does that? At least, not you, who understands the value of celebrations and the reality that a child gets only one Christmas a year.)

In my mother's book, there was no worse sin than the sin of laziness. To sit idle was to commit an offense against God.

"Lengdung, where are you?"

"I am watching TV, Mumcy."

"Nah. You shouldn't be watching TV. Come and take these beans and peel."

A few minutes later. "Mumcy, I am done peeling the beans."

"Have you washed plates?"

"Yes, Ma."

"How about your clothes, have you washed them?"

"Yes, Ma."

"Have you arranged them and put them in the bag well?"

"Yes."

"I thought your dad told you to cut the grass in the afternoon?"

"Yes, I have done that."

"Alright. Then go to Maman Zingit's house and ask her if she has any work for you."

Mother was like that. To sit idle was to violate a sacred law of being human.

In my final year of primary school, I returned home for the third term holiday, which would last about six weeks. Mother said, "You can't stay in my house idle for that long. Find out what business you want to do and let me know."

Her favorite option was hawking food items. We had done it before as kids, and I hated it. The reason I hated it is the very reason my mother loved it. It was embarrassing. Mother often said, "You can't make money if you are not shameless. Hawking will make you shameless. It will present you to people at your lowest, and if they see you that way, you will never be proud again. They will have nothing against you to look down upon, as you are already down." Her wisdom made sense for an adult, but as a kid, she was reducing my steeze (a Nigerian term for prestige).

So this time, I didn't want to hawk. I wanted something different.

It occurred to me that shoe cobbling was a viable option. My friends and I used to play on the mountains and rocks around Jenta, which often damaged our shoes. We were heading to a cobbler to repair our shoes almost every week. I realized I could corner this market of my friends. I told Mother I would open a shoe-shiner stand, as it was commonly called. She asked if I was sure that was what I wanted. I affirmed. She bought the essential tools and sent me off. Every morning, I would open my shop and wait for customers. To my surprise, my friends didn't patronize me. I expected them to, but they only came to me when they didn't have money to pay for my services. After a week, I gave up on that market and decided to go visit house by house to ask if they had shoes that needed repair.

Out of pity for me and friendship with my mother, some families brought out their shoes for me to repair. However, it was the fathers who saved my enterprise. "Well done, my boy," they would say, "you are doing well. Look at your mates playing, but you are making use of yourself. You should keep at it. Come and take my shoes to repair. On Sunday, come and shine my shoes."

Each time I returned home with some money, Mother would be proud of me. She bought me an *asusu*, a piggy bank. With the words from the fathers and the joy on my mother's face, it was tempting to see shoe-shining as my career. All I wanted to do was please my mother, and now I was. For two months, we didn't have any misunderstandings. There were no quarrels or beatings, mostly because I rarely stayed home and had no free time to be truant. On Sundays, I returned to those houses to shine shoes. Father taught me that a real man shines his shoes until he can see his face in the reflection. I went into shoe-shining with the same mindset. The fathers in the community loved this and would often overpay for my service. By the end of the holiday, I had gathered quite a sum. When the time came to break my asusu, Mother and I sat in the living room like Manager and Founder balancing the books of their giant corporation. We counted all the savings, which amounted to a few thousand naira. Mother declared that that was the money I would resume school with. She took it and kept it. When the time came, she gave me my money. I resumed school with the money I had worked for. My sweat, effort, and experience made me want to earn more. Once you make your first cash, there is no going back. You want to make more and more. Of course, I was proud of myself.

For a Nigerian woman, my mother was exceptional. She refused to be confined by traditional roles, she would partake in meetings that were designed for men only, and she would challenge many societal perception of gender roles. She was effective in everything she undertook. Our home used to be a full home. There were always relatives staying with us or someone visiting. Many people consulted her for advice on different things. Over the years, she built her reputation as a tough woman who understood business and faith. A serious Christian, she was once an elder in the Church, the Women's Fellowship Leader, and was involved in Choir, New Life For All, and Girls' Brigade. It was through the New Life For All group that she would later travel to Cameroon to preach the gospel. Mother was a woman who believed that she could manage everything. She never let anything get out of control. Perhaps that is also why she thought none of us could become wayward.

Being born in Jenta is an automatic threat to the full development of a child's potential. Teenage pregnancy, drug abuse, and all the vices you can think of in a poor ghetto community were threats that were lurking to take your child from you. While it is true that one has to choose to engage in these, Jenta is an environment that makes that choice easy. It is the default state of the community. In such an environment, it is no surprise that parents are paranoid about their children. Mother believed only the church could prevent us from going the "way of the world."

She encouraged us to participate in every church activity (even though it was not optional). However, encouragement was not adequate for me. Next, she cajoled me to join in these activities. Again, cajoling didn't work. Then she forced me. She commanded me to join every group. And this time, I complied. In my years in the church, I got involved in the Choir, Boys' Brigade, Youth Fellowship, New Life for All, Sunday School, and Shata. All these before the age of thirteen. These groups within the church have different activities on different days. Inevitably, I was in the church every day. Soon, the church held no fascination for me. I was only attending to meet friends and to wait for the activities to be over so I could visit some places my mother would disapprove of before finally getting home.

While this method did not ensure that I became an upright kid, it at least inculcated some crucial values in me. I admit this was Mother's best way of protecting me. What else could she have done? The church was everything to her and the whole community. Churches in ghettos are often the best hope of everyone there. Looking at my life and the lives of friends who didn't get involved with drugs or activities that hampered us, I see that the church was a pivotal factor. It was the place we went to instead of going to the "jungle." The jungle is an area of Jenta that has become a hangout for drug abuse and a meeting point for gangsters. Community members, especially women, avoid the jungle.

Mother built her reputation from her successful business, which was an inspiration to many. Because she was successful, other people who had business ideas or were already running their businesses sought her out. She offered advice on everything from family to business to spiritual matters. One thing about her was that she never ignored the actions of others she did not approve of. Today, we'd say she was intolerant, but I doubt if that was it. She was genuinely interested in others and wanted them to be their best. Even if she were passing by and saw a woman she did not know ineffectively selling an item, she would stop and correct her. She always received appreciation for this tutoring. I don't recall ever hearing anyone reject her advice. Most people don't want to hear criticism, even constructive. But she gave it in a way that the recipients saw the love in it.

A case I will never forget is a woman who had just gotten married. Her husband was a known philanderer and was always out of town. She sought my mother for advice on what to do since her husband was rarely present to care for the family. Mother gave her some money to start a small business. Within a few months, she had grown her business remarkably. Mother told her to purchase land. She did. A few years later, she built a house with income from the business she started with Mother's little investment. Mother would be proud of her, for Mother did not live long enough to see her reach these heights.

That's what Mother lived for: ensuring others attained the highest heights they could. She supported students with school fees, relatives with education, and community members with their businesses. She opened our home to everyone. Our house was like a small restaurant. There was always food in excess. Mother cooked enough so that there would be leftovers in case someone stopped by. Many did stop by and ate their fill.

For me, it was not the food she shared that stood out. She could see potential in everyone she came across. Mother would select some relatives from the village, bring them to the city, and ensure they got an education. She was a firm believer in education. In fact, both of my parents became ardent supporters of education. Perhaps it was because they were conscious of how the lack of it had limited their lives. Mother always said, "I will sell my last wrapper to ensure you attend the best school. You must go to the best school."

She meant it. Indeed, I got to attend the best schools.

Despite all these heroic qualities, Mother was only a human being. She had her faults. She could be brash and overbearing, demanding excellence in circumstances where it was not possible. The full consequences of her demands appeared in the relationship between her and one of my aunties, Aunty Paula, who stayed with us. Aunty Paula lived in our household for several years, tending to Mother's businesses and helping with Mother's kids. According to family folklore, Mother did the birthing of the babies while Aunty Paula did the rearing. She was instrumental in our family life, yet Mother was overbearing towards Aunty Paula. She expected so much from her; any mishap was dealt with sternly. Much worse, Mother didn't support Aunty Paula going to school. As a teenager, Aunty Paula was often teased due to her inability to communicate in English. To speak English was a mark of civility. She wanted to be civilized, but Mother was not thinking that way. Mother didn't see the long-term value of education at the time since she was herself uneducated. She believed business was a better path for Aunty Paula.

One day, Aunty Paula packed her things and ran away to the village, and never returned. It was nearly twenty years before she finally spoke to me about it. Aunty Paula explained that Mother eventually came to see her error and apologized. She added that Mother tried to make up for it by supporting her in the years after their reconciliation. There must be limits to how tough one can be in such circumstances. Mother learned that by experience.

Looking back, I see much more than what Mother taught us; how she lived influenced us the most. There is a saying, "For a Christian kid, there are five testaments: Matthew, Mark, Luke, John, and a Christian Mother." I had all five!

Mother's primary occupation was business. She was a saleswoman par excellence. A strategist of great skill. She dabbled in several trades, from selling clothes to selling food items, all with grace, making trade appear simple. It was not, I know, because we've tried several times in her absence. Her businesses were the primary source of income for the family. Due to how vital her businesses were to the family's upkeep, Father would always give her his salary, and she would pump it back into the business. Her business was always thriving. Of course, there were a few setbacks. For instance, in 2008, a crisis of religious violence in Jos made her move her primary business station from Kwararafa Market, a bustling commercial center, to Jenta Adamu, the community where we lived. The shop at Jenta Adamu became the place where Mother expected us kids to sell her wares. During holidays I was expected to spend time there.

Nothing is more dreadful for a kid than being instructed to stay in a single place and perform a monotonous task. I dreaded being told, "Go to the shop in Jenta Adamu." However, my perception of the shop changed when I met a seller who was hawking storybooks. He had small storybooks, most of which were between thirty to fifty pages. I asked Mother to purchase some for me, and she did. I enjoyed them and asked for more, and she did again. We continued this for several weeks until school resumed. Those little storybooks were books that every kid would love; stories about tortoises, rabbits, and the animal kingdom. They were seeds that laid the groundwork for books in my mind. Little did I know that books would become my life's work, and that I would be a part of a movement that distributes such books to children in Jenta.

Aunty Paula

Every family has a family historian. This person is the living embodiment of all that has been. She is there at all the significant events that shape the family. She knows all the family secrets. She knows why the bad things happened, why the good things did not happen, and why an uncle no longer visits the family. She can cause enmity between family members, and she can create a redemption path for parties in conflict. On the bright side, come what may, she serves as a bridge between generations. It is an added gift when she is a good storyteller. She tells the stories of all that has been, creating hope for what will be.

In our case, that person is Aunty Paula. (And you mustn't address her without adding the "Aunty." How dare you?)

Aunty Paula is 5'9" but as a storyteller, she stands much taller. As a fighter, she towers over most, and her heart is as high as the mountains. She loves everyone. It is no surprise that the whole family is currently built around her. Although she lives nearly one hundred thirty kilometers from the city, she is the pull that has influenced our family since my mother's absence. Some have said she inherited her attributes from our mother. It could be true. She is a ferocious fighter just like Mother; she gives without care for herself like Mother, she loves to be around people like Mother, and, like Mother, she never avoids a confrontation.

When Aunty was twelve years old, a decision was made without her input that she would go to the city to live with my mother. She arrived in 1991. For the next ten years, Aunty lived with Mother. Some thought she was Mother's first daughter. They called Mother "Maman Paula," Paula's Mother. During her stay, she learned Mother's trades. She learned to handle accounting. She learned to sell. She learned to manage people and to be as wise as a serpent. The serpent instinct was quite valuable for a teenage girl who ran a business that many adults were failing at. Mother was a great delegator with an eagle eye. To her credit, she knew how to choose the right person for the right job. Or maybe it was just that she delegated the task and entrusted the people with so much confidence that they had to get the job done. Paula got most of the job done. Mother traveled long distances to purchase goods for her stores, thus leaving Paula to run the family. On getting up in the morning, she would do the house chores, get my siblings ready for school, and afterward put me on her back to begin marching to Kwararafa, the marketplace. She would sell goods such as rice, beans, yam, potatoes, and other foodstuffs at the market. She was so good that customers trusted her in my mother's absence. In the years that Paula stayed with my family, the family moved five times.

Although she had not completed her secondary education, staying in the store refined her math skills. Mother had zero tolerance for using calculators. She would scold her, saying, "You have the same brain as the man who invented the calculator, so use your brain." As you can imagine, this was not fun for a fifteen-year-old who had to calculate numbers in hundreds of thousands. Yet, this experience fortified her skills so much that decades later, she still hates calculators and adds up numbers faster than anyone I know. When I visit a store with her, she adds the numbers so fast that she reaches the final sum before the store owner with a calculator. Twice, she saved store owners from undercharging us with her exceptional abilities.

Aunty was present at some events that even my parents missed. In 1993, when Mother gave birth to Lurit, their third child, Father was 190 kilometers away in Dogon Dutse. He was running a farm, his primary occupation at the time. Lurit was sickly from birth. For one and a half years, she was a constant visitor to the hospital. It was after treatments, injections, every form of medicine, and much trial and error that we learned she suffered from sickle cell anemia.

One day, in her 20th month, Lurit began to convulse and was taken to the hospital. Before arriving, she gave up the ghost. This was the 1990s in Nigeria; telephones were scarce, communications were still traditional, and word of mouth was the most available tool to illiterate families. Unfortunately, Father's location was so remote that few ever traveled there. Months later, when he returned from Dogon Dutse, where his farm was, he learned what had happened. For a whole year, he did not know that his daughter had died. I can only imagine how it must have hurt him. Another son was born in 1995. He lived for a few months and then died. This time around, Mother had gone to the market while Father was at home. In both cases, Paula was present.

While Paula served Mother and Father faithfully, her primary desire was to attend school like other girls her age. She was hurt each time they attended church service, and the other girls her age spoke impeccable English. At the same time, she struggled to construct a proper sentence. Even worse, the girls mocked her for this. In her mind, this also limited the kind of boyfriend she could attract. The educated ones would attract the educated ones, and all that would be left would be the uneducated ones. When two uneducated ones marry, the chances of a continuous family of uneducated children increase. She never wanted that. So, despite the beautiful relationship she had with my mother, it was a relationship with a strain.

Mother believed Paula was a talented businesswoman. Therefore, she should learn to do business rather than go to school. After all, business was feeding the family at that time. And so Mother did all she could to stop Paula from going to school. It was a decision she would come to regret. This conflict drove a wedge between Paula and Mother. Two strong personalities, with different ambitions and different priorities. It was a textbook recipe for conflict, and there would be no resolution. One day, Paula woke up, got everyone dressed for school, greeted my elder brother, a sickle cell victim lying in bed sick, wished him quick health, and told him goodbye. He asked her where she was going, but she didn't respond. She left the house that day and never returned, at least never as the same person. On reaching her grandparent's house, she declared that she would never return to my mother again.

And so it was.

Many years passed, and Aunty Paula went on to get married to an educated lecturer who supported her in completing her own education and getting a Higher National Diploma, which is equivalent to a degree. But before she left Mother, she had accumulated a substantial history of our family. I owe her for most of the knowledge of what happened before I was born. She also inherited many of my mother's attributes, such as her fierceness, zero tolerance for incompetence, and a strong sense of duty to family and society. These attributes would never leave her and would become the bond that would keep us connected with our relatives for many years after our mother died.

Aunty's full name is Paulina, which means "small," but she is not small in any way.

These people shaped me and gave me a view of everything I knew in my first few years of childhood. My life was an extension of theirs, their stories, their love, their hopes, and their lifestyle. They provided me with a crucial foundation to help me return home someday. My family was stable in my early years, which mattered almost more than anything, for a stable home was a necessity for a child's development. The gift of stability, especially in a society like Jenta, became apparent years later when I realized that very few had it. I could return "home" only because my parents had built a "home." For many kids in Jenta, there was no home. Are we surprised that many of these kids turned out to be burdens to society? Home is not just a location; it is also people who love you and the people you love. I knew I was loved, and I loved them, too.

CHAPTER 2

LITTLE LENGDUNG

Pounded yam was only prepared on special occasions, making it a special dinner. Everyone returns home on time on the day pounded yam is to be made. The elder sister pounds for Baba and Mumcy, and everyone else pounds his share. Pounded yam accompanies one of the country's most famous dishes, *egusi* soup, made from blended melon seeds and vegetables. I developed a deep appreciation for pounded yam and continue to rate it as one of humanity's best inventions. The only downside of pounded yam dinner is that by the following day, there are no leftovers. In the case of leftovers, *tuwo,* a delicacy made from cassava eaten alongside the egusi soup, always wins. Dear God, thank you for leftover tuwo and all the sweet tastes we enjoy in the morning.

But...

As a child, you must go to school every Monday through Friday. On Saturday, you are to wash your clothes and do house cleaning. On Sunday, you attend church service and enjoy Sunday rice. Apart from the festivals, Sunday is the best day every week! Best day. Favorite. Why? No matter how bad things get, you would find rice at home or at the home of one of your neighbors. A terrible Sunday is one without Sunday rice. The worst punishment parents can impose on their children is to cook something other than rice on Sunday, something like tuwo. Tuwo was a constant feature for dinner. Every dinner was tuwo—every single dinner. If things are difficult economically, the surest indicator is to see if there is tuwo. If there is no tuwo, things are very, very bad for that family. The great advantage of tuwo is that you can mold it into a solid form to eat with soup or use it to make a hot, runny pudding for break-fast or dinner. It 'stays' longer in the stomach, so every mother is sure to have tuwo no matter what. The result is that tuwo is always produced for dinner. I came to hate tuwo because it became a constant.

In every home in Jenta, you can be sure to encounter tuwo. You see it at all times, in all variations. Mother realized it was the best way to hold us hostage whenever we failed to perform tasks. She would declare with joy on her face, "You shall be eating tuwo today." Tuwo became a punish-ment. Other times, she would threaten us and say, "Will you wash these plates, or do you want to eat tuwo tonight?" The choice was obvious.

At All Nations Academy, the boarding school I attended, the pres-ence of tuwo became even more pronounced. It was the dinner meal every day of the week. There was no chance of escaping it. At least back home, there were days when dinner could vary. But in school, it was the same thing every day of the week. To make it worse, we ate it like our lives depended on it. Indeed, our lives did depend on it. By the time I finished secondary school, I was done with tuwo. I wanted nothing to do with it. I hated it, hated what it represented, and hated its presence.

Color Red

Our primary school was close to a major highway in Jos. We had traffic wardens whose responsibility was to guide students and help them with crossing the road. However, these traffic wardens were Nigerian govern-ment employees. So they arrived when civil servants were supposed to report for work, much later than when classes began at the school. One day, we got to school and saw the staff turning away students. What happened? There had been a fatal accident involving some of our students. A truck was speeding down the road when it hit about five of them; none survived. All the passengers in the vehicle also died.

Blood covered the road in front of the school gate. From then on, I began associating death with the color red. Seeing these pupils' death did not fill me with sadness as much as it filled me with fear—the fear of red.

Many years later, I realized the color of love was also red. One time, we had a special Valentine's Day celebration in church, and they compelled everyone to buy a gift for someone of the opposite gender. A girl bought me flowers in red, a red card, and the whole package in a red bag. I was puzzled by the gift until an older adult in the family told me red meant love. I could not understand how humans could associate love with red. My binary childhood mind could not accept this dichotomy.

Being an adult is being able to hold two seemingly contradictory thoughts simultaneously. Fire can be used to cook a meal, and at the same time, it can be used to burn a house down. Water can be used to quench thirst and can also be a cause of death. One cannot separate these concepts; they must be viewed from both sides. You have to live with their coexistence or be driven to paralysis by trying to insist on only one view of it.

Bathrooms

Our primary school had bathrooms for boys and girls close to each other. You would pass the girls' bathroom before getting into the boys' bathroom. Boys often stopped at the girls' bathroom and did their thing. It was a serious offense in a school such as ours. Religion and discipline were most important. But since they rarely caught us, it wasn't an issue.

I urgently had to pee one day and rushed out to use the bathroom. As usual, I stopped at the girls' bathroom. Unfortunately for me, a janitor was moving around trying to clean up the mess made by younger girls. I froze and realized I had only one option: run out quickly and hope the janitor wouldn't recognize me. I ran, but I slipped and fell hard in a pool of pee and poo. I was such a mess that the cleaner chose not to report me.

As a kid, nothing was more shameful than being thought of as someone who stained their clothes while doing their thing. It was a sign of maturity when you did everything neatly. That day, I received no cane strokes; I was wearing my punishment. I couldn't explain that I was running out of the bathroom, slipped, and got stained; no one would have believed me.

Food for thought: Shortcuts don't always lead to the desired destination.

Crossing the River

Soon, my sister joined me in primary school. My parents had determined that we all must attend Police Children School, a primary school run by the Nigerian Police Force's Directorate of Police Education, if only for family tradition. My sister was a slow walker, as a schoolboy would expect of a girl. She slowed me down whenever we were going to school. It's a longstanding community tradition for the older kids to help the younger kids when going to school. Oma did the same for us until she graduated; Vero did the same for us until she graduated; and Peter did the same for us until he graduated.

Now, it was my turn.

Between our home and school is a long river crossing almost the whole city of Jos. When it rains, the river floods to its bank, and those on the road have to use a single bridge that allows entrance into Jenta. Going by this route makes the journey longer.

The rains had come that day. However, we were too tired to go the long way via the bridge route. We wanted to take the usual shortcut. That day, there were five of us coming home from school. When we got to the river, the waters were high: not too high for the older kids but definitely too high for the younger.

One of the older kids, Esson, and I devised a plan. I would stand in the middle of the river, and he would pass each younger kid to me so I could drop them off on the other side. The younger kids were all afraid, but we convinced them by using encouraging words and crossing the river ourselves. We passed the first young kid, and it was a success. We did the same for the second; it was successful, too. The third one was where all hell broke loose. I did not hold her firmly enough, so she slipped into the water. The river water was dirty and red and contained many harmful objects due to the heavy rain flow. This water was going to take her if we didn't act fast. I dived immediately, grabbed her, and passed her to Esson on the other side. We knew that when we got home, and the story leaked, our parents would scold and punish us for insisting on following a dangerous route. Some kids have been lost due to such experiences. We had received many warnings before then. The kid we saved, Ufungil, did not return to our band. We didn't need to ask her why.

Life is like Pneumonia

There was a day in class when our Health Education teacher, Mr. Kabiru, walked to the board and wrote a word on it. He said anyone who could pronounce it correctly would receive a monetary reward. The word was PNEUMONIA.

I was in Primary 3, and I had never seen that word in my life. None of us in the class had. So, how would we pronounce this word that starts with P N. We tried hard, but none of us got it. We were pronouncing it precisely as it appeared, with the P and N coming out clearly. Thinking about it now, it was hilarious. By the end of that class, we had learned the correct pronunciation of pneumonia. We laughed at ourselves for our earnest, though completely wrong, attempts. But even after I knew how to say it, something kept bothering me. Why was this word pronounced so differently from how it looked? Why write it one way and say it another? It felt like a strange trick of the language, and it got me thinking: maybe this is how life works, too. Things aren't always as they appear on the surface. Sometimes, what you see isn't the whole story—you must dig deeper and look beyond appearances to understand how things are. Just like with that word, life often hides its meaning in unexpected places, and only by being open to learning can we uncover the truth beneath the surface.

Wanderings

Another way we spent time during these childhood and teenage years was in our endless wanderings. We would wander away to anywhere. We would leave home and head to nowhere at all. We would visit different communities that could be as far as five drops by motor transport. We had no mission, friends, or relatives in these communities and no specific place to go. We just wanted to go somewhere else that wasn't home. New areas were exciting. We loved the idea of just leaving home and discovering new places. While this filled us with a feeling of adventure, it filled our parents with dread. Such escapades caused some kids to get lost, and to this day, no one has found them.

The biggest thrill in these adventures was climbing onto trucks that supplied Jenta with sand or cement. We would get on these trucks and go wherever they led. Sometimes, they would carry us to the highway. At such times, we might see someone in the community that recognized us. They would shout at us, telling us to drop down, but we rarely did. It would take a beating to get us down. On the way home, other people on the road would shout at us, too, threatening a beating or some other punishment. None of that bothered us. If anything, we enjoyed the shouting; it was all part of the game, pushing the limits and breaking the rules.

We couldn't always wait for a truck to take us on these adventures, so we crafted homemade skateboards with four small tires and a wooden board. This board could move if we stood on it with one leg and kicked with the other. It could not take you far, but you could have an exciting ride if you grabbed onto a car. What thrills we got! Of course, no car owner wanted us hanging onto his car. So it was the same game of hide and seek all over again. If we were caught, the punishment was severe. But we were rarely apprehended.

We soon understood that you could get away with anything; the only thing was to ensure you were never caught. Avoiding risks and problems was not the motto of our lives; avoiding being caught was the motto. That's how we lived.

Fights were also a regular part of our lives, inter-community fights especially. Jenta vs Gada Biu, Jenta vs Barracks, Jenta vs Angwan Rogo. It was a defining characteristic of Jenta. Our reputation preceded us. It became so bad that other communities refused to participate in competitions with Jenta. Jenta citizens could fight for any reason and at any event. At parties, ceremonies, picnics, church programs, trade fairs, and the most consuming activity of all: football. Football was the medium that led to many fights.

Often, when we went to football matches, we got the team of players ready and another team in parallel. This second team had only one objective: to fight. They were often bulky, drug users, and stupidly bold. They were the kind of guys hired by politicians to serve as thugs. In our case, we didn't need to pay them. They just loved Jenta and the reputation they had built for themselves as tough guys.

If a match was going well, they served as cheerleaders. If a game was going badly, they would get on with their mission. They would begin by finding fault in the referee's calls. They would then proceed to say provoking things. If the others were less inclined to fight, they would begin the fight themselves. When fights began, the game would come to an end. Rather than lose, the game would be declared inconclusive. We did this so many times other communities soon learned our tricks and began bringing their team of thugs, too. Sometimes, the quarrels would get bloody.

We didn't want to be defeated, especially when we could do something about it, even if it was unfair and stupid. Negative attitudes fueled our actions. We didn't want to accept the world the way it was. We didn't want to agree that we were losers. We already knew we were losers just by being born in Jenta and staying there, but we didn't want anyone to tell us that. We would stand up to fight and reject any such verdicts. Our fights were reactions against this. We thought it was the only way we could cope with the world.

Football

I wanted to be Ronaldinho one day. The next day, I wanted to be Kaka. The next day, I wanted to be Luis Figo. It was endless. It was the football dream. Every kid in Jenta played football. Football was not just a game but a hobby, an addiction, and a culture. Kids who didn't play football were only the rare ones who didn't have the talent for it.

As young boys, football dominated our lives. It was the one sport we could play despite Jenta's limitations. All you needed to enjoy the game was to have two people. Even one person could enjoy dribbling the ball. We played football during our school break, after school, in the evening, well into the night, and every time we were allowed to. It was an obsession, an obsession that affected our responsibilities as kids. As kids, we were responsible for washing plates, sweeping the compound, fetching water, and running errands. Football constantly interrupted these.

I never did become a professional footballer. However, as a boy, I was good at the game and thus was always on the first list of any match. I was light, slim, and always funny. I could easily navigate the opposition's defenses. I fancied becoming a professional footballer someday. I dreamed that one day, I would play for the big clubs and become an international figure like Jay Jay Okocha or Nwankwo Kanu, two Nigerians who had made their names in the sport.

I had a cousin who fueled this dream: Jukgak Goma, who was nearly twice my age. He was a famous grassroots footballer. He was known all over the city as a very talented player. Just saying, "I am Jukgak's brother," earned me some respect and set expectations. Jukgak had been one of the few players from Jenta who had built a reputation as a professional player. He had traveled to some foreign countries like Turkey and Togo, as well as some European countries. He had played for Pepsi Football Academy for some years. I idolized him. Each time I saw him, I felt, "Oh yes, someone is doing it so I can, too." As I grew up, I lived on the stories of his travels. There were many medals in his room, trophies, and posters that made a statement. Those relics were a big inspiration to me. It was as though football and I were a match made in heaven.

One popular tournament that exists to this day is the Plateau Radio Television Under-15 5-Aside Football tournament, a football competition for boys under the age of fifteen. At least eight teams comprising five players competed in the tournament for weeks. The excitement that built up before the event and the popularity of the star players after the tournament was incredible. Although my team never won, it was always delightful to be a part of. I participated in the tournament each year until I had to leave for secondary school in a different local government area.

For the Girls

As a teenager, nothing is desired more than an opportunity to display your talents or skills before the opposite gender. My opportunity came in my final year at primary school. The game was football, and the field was one of the most famous fields in Jos, Police Field, just behind our school. We played football daily during our break time, but this was different. It was a send-off match for the final-year pupils. I had told my mother about it and pestered her to get me football shoes. Partly because she never supported my football dreams and partly because she didn't understand football, she got me shoes with more foam than cotton. The kind that would get soaked and burden the wearer when exposed to water.

I prayed hard that it wouldn't rain on D-day. When the day came, there was no rain in the morning. By 11 AM, we marched out to the field. The games began at 11:30 AM, and by 11:40 AM, it started to rain. A few minutes later, I was substituted into the game. I touched the ball only once throughout my nearly thirty minutes in the game. My soaked shoes hindered me. That game was supposed to display my skills to the girls; instead, it showed them how incompetent I was. It was the shoes, not me, but who cares? For kids, you were either good or not. I wasn't good that day, and it became my reputation until graduation.

David vs Goliath

One day in my final year of primary school, I met Murphy, a close neighbor, after classes. As we were walking home, he mentioned that he would be stopping by a place I might want to see. I followed him. On arriving, I saw boys with controllers in their hands, their eyes locked on a TV screen, and they were having the time of their lives. Curious, I watched for some minutes, and then he asked me to take the controls. I tried my first game. It was called Winning Eleven, and he beat me by a score of 14:0. He told me my session was over. Damn! I had just had the most fun I'd had in all my life. I ran home, stole money from Mother's shop, and returned to the game house. I didn't leave until late in the evening. By the end of that day, I was thoroughly initiated. For the next six years, I would be a game addict, stealing from Mother's shop (often getting caught and punished) to fulfill my desires. I played every game available to kids from my part of the world: Shaolin Monk, God of War, Need for Speed, PES, Winning Eleven, Teken, and MK Armageddon.

Theft aside, I became a reputable game champion in the community, and other boys respected me for my game prowess. They knew I was a champion and began to dread playing against me. I knew all the game palaces in Jenta. Everywhere I went, the first thing I asked about was the location of the game palace. It is fitting that we called those places "Game Palaces." We, the peasants, brought our little wealth to the game kings; we helped them maintain their palaces at our expense.

When I got to secondary school, my reputation as a "strong hand" in the game remained undiminished. A new boy arrived at our school and was in the limelight for a few weeks. He was a loudmouth. He told everyone that he was the GOAT (Greatest Of All Time) of games. He had competed against many players and had beaten them. One night, we got the chance to compete. That night, he raved again, telling everyone who cared to listen what a champ he was. In a stupid show of bravado, I agreed to play with him. We left school that night and got to town at about 8:00 PM. Unfortunately for him, I beat him several times that day with unquestionable scores. That day, my reputation reached the roof. And he? How the mighty had fallen.

I was proud of myself. Everyone was. I had just silenced a Goliath.

My favorite game in those days was Mortal Kombat Armageddon. It's an adventure game where two parties can play; I always loved it when there were two. The fighters journey through different stages with a major villain in each stage. Shao Kang is the final villain, but I never beat him, which is something I still hold against myself. Maybe someday.

Life was good. It was fun. I lived for every moment. I had no understanding of the world at a deep level, no understanding of responsibilities, and no one expected much from me. My inability to defeat Shao

Kang was a harbinger of things to come. My childhood was interrupted abruptly, leaving many things unfinished. As I moved to Bokkos for secondary school, my interest in PlayStation waned. I spent most of my time in a boarding house that had little space for such things. When I had the chance to return to this formerly pleasurable activity, there was no way I could afford it. A tragic event happened in my family, bringing hard times where simply affording three meals a day was the highest priority. That change upended the world as I knew it.

CHAPTER 3

JENTA

One of the worst things about growing up in a slum like Jenta is that it destroys your self-esteem. You live your whole life unsure of your identity, potential and abilities. You are always wondering if you will ever reach the standards of others, others who are better than you in your eyes. Looking at the world through this lens, one inevitably struggles with everything. However, I was lucky that this mindset didn't consume me, although I struggled for years whenever I had to meet with kids and adults from other areas. When we attended events, I was self-conscious about my shoes, my clothes, my everything. In my mind, I would never measure up. I would never reach their level. Just by being from Jenta, I was already disqualified. This disqualification was reinforced by the comments of others about me, and other kids from Jenta. One episode remains fresh in my memory.

In our final year at primary school, an NGO visited with a request. The school was to submit the names of its three best students, and they would participate in promoting peace in Plateau State. The concept was that kids would role-play as government officials and make declarations to ensure their generation's peace. They needed kids who were bright and could deliver speeches. The school chose Chidubem (Assistant Head Boy), another pupil, and me to participate. During rehearsals, they taught us how to role-play and deliver speeches effectively. When we got to the rehearsal venue on the first day, the organizers asked us to introduce ourselves and mention our names, school, current position in class, and the name of our street. It got to my turn:

"My name is Lengdung Apolos Tungchamma from Police Children School, Jos Main. I took first position last year. I live in Jenta."

"Jenta?" one of the staff retorted.

I replied, "Yes."

He just moved on with a sigh of disappointment. It was the first time I had experienced other people's attitudes towards my community. His face wore an expression of hopelessness. The implications of my being from Jenta went beyond his sigh.

The mock government contained various positions: the Governor, the Deputy Governor, the Secretary to the Government, the Commissioner for Education, the Commissioner of Police, etc. We were to be assigned these roles depending on our academic performances. Two of us had gotten the first position in our schools, so the staff were supposed to decide which of us would become the Governor. But there was nothing to decide. One staff member boldly said, "A child from Jenta cannot act as Governor." That was that. They appointed the other boy the Governor, and I was appointed the Commissioner of Police.

What had just happened? I had just been disqualified from being a Governor due to my geography. Just for being from Jenta? Why? Was Jenta that bad? The verdict from the outside world was "yes." Jenta was that bad, and being from Jenta eliminated you from specific opportunities. You did not deserve the respect, the privileges, or the responsibilities that others deserved.

A person from Jenta was a nobody. They were on the wrong side of the world.

As I grew older, this stigma became more pronounced. Whenever I would attend a program and have to introduce myself with, "My name is Lengdung Apolos Tungchamma, from Jenta," people's expressions would change immediately. Any acceptance there may have been previously, vanished. Suspicion became the order of the day. I saw this stigma everywhere. In Terminus, the central business hub of Jos city, there is a sort of embargo by the business owners against Jenta citizens. When you look for a job and introduce yourself as a person from Jenta, it becomes harder to get the job.

To be fair, some of the judgment of Jenta was understandable, due to the prevalent vice and crime. But just because a boy had the misfortune of being born in Jenta didn't make him a criminal.

Castle In The Valley

Jenta is a valley filled with massive blocky boulders heaped on each other as if Picasso himself had arranged them. The negative spaces of the rugged rocky terrain are filled with homes packed together like sardines. After the rainy season, green fills the area with color, making it strikingly beautiful. At the heart of Jenta Mangoro is a mighty rock that stretches to the sky. You can see the entire community's glory and poverty from that vantage point. The houses are nearly identical, united by the faded color of rusting tin roofs, signifying poverty and age. You can see the streets, the roads, and the people going about their activities.

It is a small land area with few public places: the football field, churches, schools, viewing centers, game palaces, and beer parlors. There are many beer parlors and only a few schools. Sometimes, I can't help but imagine what would happen if Jenta had schools in place of the beer parlors. I might never know.

Jenta did not have a swimming pool, but we did not need one. We had a river that was full of life. The river's flow was not just the flow of water; it was also the flow of our lives. Close to the river was a football field that allowed us to play football "until Mama calls." The river was where we got water for bathing and home cleaning. It was also the place where we learned to swim. Cultural norms divided the river, one side for the men and the other side for the women. The men's side had a shallow part and a deep part. We called the deep part "Gidan Boss," House of the Boss. An older boy would pick up a younger boy and drop him into the center of Gidan Boss to learn to swim. From there, he would begin his life as a swimmer: no manuals, no introduction, no conclusion, and no lifeboat. Of course, most people nearly drowned the first time.

On my first day as a swimmer, an older boy unceremoniously cast me into the deep. As soon as he released me, I started shouting. With every shout, water entered my mouth. I wasn't only shouting; I was splashing wildly, creating chaos. Water was entering my nose. It was as though water was entering my whole body via every opening. I ran out of strength and was slowly reducing my efforts. It was then that an older boy dragged me to the river bank. My eyes were red; I couldn't see or hear clearly. They told me, "Welcome to the club." Out of sheer desire to be amongst the big boys, I didn't quit. I returned the next day and started with the shallow area. It was from here that I learned to swim. It was a breeze when I got to try it years later in a swimming pool.

The Ones Ruined

The most essential part of childhood is helping a child avoid choices that could ruin their future. In a sane society, various structures, from social groups to community organizations, ensure that the child does not do this.

Jenta was not that kind of place.

When I got older and reflected on my friends whose lives went south, it began with the absence of such structures. Some began to miss school, and their parents were too busy to notice and ensure they attended. Teachers had too many students in a class to see that one student was missing. And society was generally indifferent to schooling. To them, "Who school epp?" meaning, schooling is not helpful.

No one illustrates this more than my friend Adam. We grew up in the same neighborhood; we played football together, ran the streets together, hunted mangoes, and swam together. He was older than I, but I was better academically. The classroom was a prison cell to him; every day, he looked for an opportunity to miss class. He got many opportunities to miss classes by pretending to be sick, or running an errand for his father, or pretending to lack one thing that would keep him out of school. When the session ended, his results often showed he ranked among the poorest in the class. This is where I came in.

He would bring the results to me, and I would carefully forge the document, editing his position in class and placing him in an average position that wouldn't put him in trouble. His parents were largely indifferent. This routine continued for many years until he reached the final year of secondary school when he had to write the West African Senior School Certificate Examination (WASSCE). This examination, consisting of nine subjects, was mandatory for senior secondary school students who intended to proceed to higher institutions after their secondary education. He took the exams, and when the results came out, he failed all nine subjects. This time, there was nothing we could do. We destroyed the result papers and exhausted the PIN usage to check the results online. When his parents asked for his results, we kept telling them they had not yet been released. Because they were not too involved in his life, they believed us and didn't follow up with the school.

A few years later, his father died, and his mother had to become the breadwinner of the family. Things became worse, and so did Adam's life. He started doing drugs and smoking. He would return home and beat his younger sisters. He was constantly quarreling with his mother, from whom he regularly stole. She was a micro business owner who barely earned $10 per day. He was in prison twice and recently was reported to be a gang member.

When I think about what went wrong with Adam's life, I think about the fact that there was no family or societal structure to prevent him from going haywire. He was just one of many friends who went that route; there are many other Adams whose stories might never be told.

Maybe I'll Become Mark Zuckerberg

The prospect of their children being consumed by Jenta's notorious thug culture was a pervasive and perpetual fear that haunted every parent in the community. Bad companions could influence your child to become a thief, a drug addict, or an obsessive footballer. For parents, every unaccounted minute away from home is a danger and calls for concern. I was always somewhere out of the house. It became such a serious problem that my parents had to find an alternative activity.

My dad was the solution provider. One day, he told me to stop by his office after school. I did, and he took me to the office of one of his friends. Mr. Isaac was in this one-room space which had three computers. I saw a man playing a Mavis Beacon typing game. I was fascinated. My dad declared that, from now on, this is where I would go after school. It was a pronouncement of punishment. But he did not know then that you can't punish a child with a computer. Instantly, I attempted to play the Mavis Beacon game. I was drunk with it. I stayed there all day and returned home late in the evening. From then on, it was clear that computers would be my life. I knew what I wanted to study in the future—Computer Science.

Many years later, his decision to punish me with computers would return to haunt him. While he would be proud of me for learning computers early, he would be confused by my decision to become a computer scientist. Like almost every parent, my dad wanted me to become a doctor or something with a "guarantee" of a good job. I had already shown a streak of academic brightness. Hence, the expectation was that I would automatically become a respected professional. Unknown to him, my days at Habi Best Computer School had soaked me in the world of computers, and I wanted to remain there. A significant turning point for me was when I learned there was this new tool that everyone was talking about: Facebook. I discovered a young American school dropout named Mark Zuckerberg had created it. Whatever the circumstances, I wanted to become like Mark Zuckerberg.

Security Question

When we returned home from school one day, we saw that somebody had painted numbers on our walls. It was 2007, and a new Governor had been sworn in. One of his top projects was numbering the houses in Plateau State. This was the first time in Jenta's history that a proper housing scheme was enacted.

"Go and copy the house address," my mother instructed.

I did.

"Say it out for me."

"No. 106 C Avenue, Jenta Mangoro."

"Say it again."

"No. 106 C Avenue, Jenta Mangoro."

"Say it two times."

I did.

"Say it five times."

I did.

"Now, never forget this number. Remember it the same way you remember memory verses. If you ever get lost, tell it to anyone you find, and they will bring you home. Do you understand?"

"Yes, Ma."

I never forgot the address and the instructions. I couldn't stop using it many years after I moved and changed addresses. Whenever I need to fill out my address on any form, I still write the same thing: "No. 106 C Avenue, Jenta Mangoro." It was my home, both physically and metaphorically. How can one outgrow a home? You can't. You add other homes.

It doesn't matter if your house was big, or small, whether it was well designed or built by amateurs, it was home. No. 106 was my home.

Looters

The actual name of my neighborhood is "Jenta Mangoro," which translates to "Jenta Mango," because there are many mango trees around us. Sadly, more and more property owners cut down the trees. As I was growing up, it was common to see children take up mango robbery. I say it was robbery, not petty theft. Real brazen robbery. The strategy involved, the risk, the action, and the consequences took it to the next level of crime. After school, children would pass through some sections of town where there are many mango trees. 'Looters' was the most popular of these places.

Looters is the name of a neighborhood adjoining the poorest and wealthiest parts of Jenta. It is an area of large compounds with high fences and several houses. Most residents were white foreigners; missionaries working in the city. As expected, they had dogs.

There was one rule of mango grabbing: never ask the owner before stealing. In most cases, the owner would give it to you for free without stress. But no, you are not supposed to ask. Where is the fun in that? Asking removes the possibility of a noteworthy criminal adventure. (By the way, I don't remember enjoying any mango that was given to me for free.) So it was usual for us to storm to Looters, steal some mangoes with utmost secrecy, and then leave without the owners knowing anyone had been there. Sometimes, we would experience hazards, one of which has been forever etched in my memory.

On this particular day, five of us went on the mango-grabbing operation. We succeeded in climbing through the fence and getting in the trees. The second phase of the operation was also a success: getting mangoes into our bags. But that was all that went according to plan. Somehow, the dog within the compound noticed us in the trees and began barking. After some minutes of mad barking, the owner came out to check. That was the moment things fell apart. Legend had it that these white men had guns in their closets and that it was these very guns that were used to conquer our forefathers. As a kid, I believed that two hundred percent. Due to the confusion, one of us fell out of the tree. The second rule of mango grabbing is never to allow yourself to get caught, no matter what. Do whatever it takes, but don't get caught.

We threw away all the mangoes we had plucked and took to our heels. Usually, we would go over the fence, but this time around, the fence option was too far. We had to go through the gate. There were only two paths to the gate; one was directly through the main door of the house and the other was blocked by a new six-foot soak-away or open sewer. In a normal circumstance on a normal day, none of us would attempt to jump that. On this day, it was different. We didn't think twice. That was our escape route. Our only escape route. I don't know how it happened, but it happened anyway. I had leaped across the soak-away and found myself breathing hard, far away from the house.

I had escaped. We had escaped. That was the critical part. How did we jump that soak-away? That day, I counted it as a miracle. Many years later, I read about the "panic monkey" who gives us the courage to do impossible things when we face impossible situations.

Ever since, I have concluded that to escape Jenta's mentality, one needs to have an effective panic monkey. Only a strong determination fueled by an external circumstance can force one to begin to think differently. This was Newton's Law of Motion: A life will remain in a state of rest or uniform motion unless an external force acts upon it. What would be my external force?

CHAPTER 4

Shoe in the River

One of the earliest memories I have as a child is of my family running away from home. One of my aunties tied me to her back, and we ran. As we ran to cross the Jenta stream, one of my shoes fell into the river. I kept crying, "Daddy, daddy, shoe fell down. Shoe there. Shoe in the river."

He paid no attention. I cried until we reached the police barracks. I kept explaining to our fellow co-travelers, who included my mother, my siblings, uncles and aunties, and some of our neighbors, that my shoe had fallen in the river. To silence me, my father said he would get the shoe for me later. I believed him but did not fully understand what was happening.

We were running away from our home because of the infamous Jos Crisis. In 2001, one of the most bitter religious conflicts in Nigeria's history engulfed the city of Jos. Some outside reports labeled it a riot; others said it was a disturbance. But for those of us who lived through it, it was war. Neighbors attacked each other with knives, machetes, and guns throughout ten days of intense conflict. In the end, according to official sources, the violence killed over a thousand people, and more than 50,000 people were displaced. It was most likely more than that. The crisis tore many families apart, and to date, some family members are still missing. For the city itself, the trauma of the situation still hangs in the atmosphere. At any loud sound, everyone takes to their heels. There are parts of Jos that Muslims cannot visit, and there are parts of Jos that Christians cannot enter. The city has been permanently divided into two sections.

It wasn't always this way.

Jos was once a melting pot of Nigeria. The city welcomed anyone from every part of Nigeria, and foreigners from other countries found homes there. Jos is a beautiful place. Situated nearly a mile high on the country's central plateau, it has mild weather and an attractive landscape with many striking rock formations and natural views that draw people from different walks of life.

Long before independence, Jos was an important British colonial city located in central Nigeria. The discovery of tin within Jos pushed the British to establish a city structure to maximize this natural resource. In time, it became a place of rest for expatriates who worked in the country and enjoyed famous tourist destinations such as Hill Station. The city served as a perfect intersection between the northern part of the country and the southern part—it was midway—a junction, a center, a melting pot. Under British rule, the city of Jos began to take shape. However, after independence, the migration of Nigerians from everywhere intensified. They came from the towns and villages. They came from the north, south, east, west, and everywhere. Muslims came. Christians came. Igbos came. Ngas came. Yoruba came. Tarok came. My father and mother also came.

As migrants arrived, they established new neighborhoods. Jenta was one such place, and my parents built a life there. They thought Jenta was one of the most beautiful new areas of Jos. It was perfect. The cost of living was affordable, and for many families—from different tribes and different religions—it was an easy place to squat until they figured things out. The squatters stayed and eventually settled in Jenta. Jenta was blessed with diversity as all these different people moved in together.

However, in 2001, its biggest blessing became the source of its biggest tragedy. Jenta became one of the most significant locations of unrest. Christians and Muslims who had lived side by side picked up machetes to attack each other. Neighbors who had shared meals during Christmas and Sallah were now shedding each other's blood. It was a period of destruction. Muslims and Christians in Jenta tried to mete out maximum damage on each other, just like what was happening all over the city. Because the population of Muslims in Jenta was smaller than the population of Christians, they overpowered the Muslims. Rumors that Muslims had been preparing for the crisis for a long time fueled the frenzy, which led to an invitation by Christians in Jenta to other Christians in other areas to come and help them "win." The result was the complete expulsion of Muslims from Jenta. Before the crisis, there had been many Muslims; after the crisis, there was not a single one.

Many years later, some Muslims returned to Jenta to sell their houses at extremely low prices. Someone would live in their house without their permission if they didn't sell. A few stayed back and converted to Christianity. They became Christians because it was the only way they could stay alive, and they chose to stay because it was the only home these pragmatic converts knew or ever had. They couldn't build or start over somewhere else. Thus, Jenta became one of the partitioned parts of Jos. In future conflicts, Christian youths from Jenta were invited to go "win" other areas as they had won Jenta in 2001. Jenta was safe... but for Christians only. Just as Angwa Rogo was safe, but for Muslims only.

My heroes in those days were men who had bows and arrows around them. I had seen them chasing Muslims while we were escaping Jenta.

To this day, one of the most vivid images in my mind is that of a group of Jenta youths who were standing on a rock, strategizing how to rush a particular Muslim house to destroy it and kill the residents. From Jenta's giant rock formations, they could see where the Muslims were and where they could attack. While the women and children escaped to the police barracks, the fathers and other young men stayed at home to defend the community.

Each time there was an attack, we ran to the barracks for safety. The 2001 crisis was the first time we went there. In the police barracks, we were refugees. We slept outside and shared meals provided by kind neighbors or purchased with whatever money we could scrape together. Father often visited us with food items, and we shared them with everyone we knew. Every day he returned, I would ask for my shoe. He would tell me he would bring it the next time. I believed him. I didn't comprehend what was going on. For me, it was like watching the movies. I had difficulty grasping that this was not a movie but real life. War movies were fun; the attacks, the killings, and the fights were entertaining. I thought it was the same here. I felt the hero could move in and out and do whatever he wanted. My father was that hero. He was supposed to be able to do everything. He was supposed to be able to provide all we needed. Only in 2008, when another crisis happened, did I fully understood what had happened in 2001. The violence was more real this time since my understanding of the world was better. War was no fun.

On November 28, 2008, we set out for school around 7:00 a.m. We were close to school when we saw people running towards us. Although we did not see what they were running from, we joined them. We ran back to a safe distance, and that's when we noticed smoke going up in the sky. Another crisis had begun.

Local government elections had just been held the previous day, and vote counting continued the following day. However, some citizens could not wait for the count to be over. Rumors began to spread that a Christian candidate was winning the polls for the seat of Jos North Local Government Chairman. Jos North is one of the LGAs comprising the capital city and is home to both Muslims and Christians. Muslim youths began rioting and destroying properties. Soon, violence engulfed the whole city. By November 30, more than seven hundred people were dead and a thousand injured. Thousands were displaced, and old wounds were reopened. It took the army days to restore order to the city.

Bombs and More Blood

For a few years, it was calm, but the tense atmosphere was palpable. Christian areas were still off-limits for Muslims, and Muslim areas were still off-limits for Christians. Suspicions toward each other bubbled under the surface as the grievances of the fathers influenced a new generation. On January 1, 2010, while the rest of the world was still celebrating the new year, the citizens of Jos were counting their dead. Another crisis had occurred, this time killing more than three hundred people. Houses were burned, along with churches, schools, and public properties. But this crisis was different in a sinister way. The combatants introduced a new element—bombs! Before 2010, bomb blasts were things we only heard of in movies. Now, they had become our reality. Two bombs exploded in Angwan Rukuba.

Previously, during a crisis, one could stay safe by running away from the danger zones or running to a predominantly Christian or Muslim area, depending on one's religion. But now, with bombs, no one was safe. In 2012, a bomb exploded in Terminus, and as people were fleeing from the scene, some ran to Gada Biu. As they reached Gada Biu, another bomb exploded. Some escaped from Terminus only to meet their death in Gada Biu. No one was safe. Bombs were everywhere: in churches, mosques, schools, markets, and just about any public place. The father of my friend and neighbor Christopher Abai was one of those running from Terminus when the bomb killed him in Gada Biu. He was a kindly community man who made friends with everyone, young and old. Everyone had fond memories of him. The bomb blew him to pieces. When we gathered for his funeral, the whole neighborhood was in tears, not just for him but for the entire city. We had never seen anything like this. Our lives would never be the same again. We were in constant fear that a bomb could explode at any moment.

The bomb blasts also radicalized many youths. They killed a suspected enemy in the slowest, most painful way when they caught him. To the youths, this was revenge for the kinds of death they were unleashing on our people. Memories of the crisis became rallying points for authority figures to build their political careers by fueling division. Their rhetoric taught us to hate our fellow citizens, never to see them as humans, and we learned well. The evidence was before us. How could we resist this?

Umar and People Like Umar

My best friend in primary school was Umar. Umar lived in Kwararafa, a post-crisis Muslim area. I could not understand why the world had to be divided along religious lines. I never understood why I should see Umar as "Muslim" instead of "friend" and why it mattered that he was Muslim and not Christian like me. At great risk, I would follow my friend Umar through Muslim-dominated areas to go to his house after school. I never felt threatened or scared. He never harmed me in any way. Maybe it was childish ignorance. I am sure kids do better at living in peace than adults.

While the traumatizing stories of Muslim and Christian neighbors turning on each other filled the Jos Crisis story, I learned of people who testified to being saved by someone of the opposite religion. There were Muslims who hid fleeing Christians in their ceilings, under their beds, and in backyards and swore by whatever they believed in that they had not seen them when the insurgents interrogated them. There were Christians who also did the same. I wish these stories were told more often and passed down like family heirlooms to the younger generation instead of the tales of betrayals and blame. Maybe the next generation would have carried on with my childlike innocence, and maybe, just maybe, we would have had less bloodshed.

While the city began to heal slowly over the years, many boundaries remained, and many wounds remained unhealed. To this day, many families still ache for closure over missing family members who never returned. Inevitably, these events forever altered my view of the world, especially of religion, through the broken lens of these bloody episodes. I asked questions. How could God allow all these things to happen? Why were people killed in the name of God? Where was God in all of this? These unanswered questions from repeated crises became part of my growing case against God.

I continued to attend church, for the society I lived in could not tolerate a person who didn't go to church. The pressure of the community made me go from Sunday to Sunday. I didn't want to be considered an outcast and didn't dare to break the bonds of tradition. However, the damage was done. I was on shaky ground. The questions were too serious to be dismissed, and they lingered in my mind for years.

The Crisis shaped us, directly and indirectly. Anyone who grew up in Jos in the 2000s, has a "Jos Crisis Story." Mine affected me in more ways than I knew. It made me aware of people outside Jenta for the first time. The Crisis also provided me with an unexpected opportunity to assert my independence.

CHAPTER 5

INDEPENDENT DECISIONS

Due to the incessant crises in Jos, a Non-Governmental Organization came up with the idea that children should be encouraged to become advocates of peace by having many of the brightest students in Jos take positions in a mock Jos government. The leadership for this pseudo-government was to be selected from various schools, including mine, which was reputable even though it was on the border of Jenta. Thus, in my final year in primary school, I was selected, along with a few other students, to be part of the "Children's Government" initiative I wrote about earlier.

Since being from Jenta had disqualified me from the office of Governor, the organizers assigned me to the position of Police Commissioner. They assumed I could easily fit that role since I was from a Police Children's School, and they were right. I was proud to be assigned to such a powerful position, and fortunately for me, I could already look the part. My school had made costume police uniforms for World Children's Day parades, and we enjoyed flaunting them. The police are a symbol of power. In a culture like ours, power means everything.

Each time we wore those uniforms, we made sure to torment boys and girls who were from other schools.

The duration of this child government program was one week. We visited a different government ministry, organization, or religious body daily. At each meeting, there would be a brief introduction where we would stand and introduce ourselves. At each place, I would say, "Good day, everyone. My name is Lengdung Tungchamma. I am the Commissioner of Police."

Boy-o-boy, it was thrilling to do that!

On the final day, we had the opportunity to meet all the actual government officials, including the Governor and his cabinet. The Commissioner of Police was there too, and suddenly, my twelve-year-old self took it very seriously. Standing before him, I looked him straight in the eye. I understood that I was meeting the real Commissioner of Police, and I needed to act appropriately to show him I hadn't misused the power of this position.

We delivered speeches depending on our location. At the Governor's office, it was the Governor. At the Ministry of Health, it was the health commissioner. I gave the speech at the police headquarters. The visits to each of these places came with some gift items. Every ministry seemed to compete to show us who was best. We brought backpacks every time and had full stomachs when we returned home. They had us eat at the best places, meet the most influential people in the state, and we got the opportunity to express our childish observations.

These thrills were not the defining part of the program for me, however; it was something else.

The schools and the NGO organizing the event reached a mutually beneficial agreement. If the program's activities caused us to miss any classes, my teachers would hold a special class time, and the NGO would compensate them for their overtime. However, as the days unfolded, the private organization was not keeping its end of the bargain. My school figured that if we were meeting government officials, it was likely that the organization was getting some money. Whether they were right or wrong, I don't know. Towards the end of our one-week escapades, my school responded by stopping all the kids from our school from attending the program until the organization agreed to meet their obligations.

Like, really? I couldn't accept this! I went home that day and resolved not to follow these instructions. The next day, I went straight to our meeting point instead of the school. Until then, the group always went to school first, and then we were driven from our school to the venue. I decided to take the rebellious path because I was sure there would be no chance of attending the program that day if I had gone to school. As I had feared, all those who had gone directly to the school could not participate that day.

My school was stunned by my rebellion. The teachers were too stunned to respond to my actions and didn't even punish me for my disobedience. When I returned to school the next day, none of my teachers confronted me about what I had done, although my mates informed me that I had enraged all of them. I never learned why they had left me alone. I think the teachers knew I did the right thing to attend the program. I had made an important independent decision.

Other than my childhood exuberance, which led to my actions, there was also a part of me that truly loved what the pseudo-government was doing. Even then, I hated the violent situation in my city. Our visits to different government agencies achieved their intended goal, contributing to my desire to advocate for peace. It was also unfair that we should miss the chance to make our voices heard due to petty differences between the controlling powers—adults.

Rite of Passage

The river is not just a water source for Jenta residents; it is also the path used to discover the many excitements of the teenage years. It was where you caught up with the latest stories in the hood, where you saw your crush, and where the older kids introduced younger ones to some practices of the underbelly of Jenta.

On the path to the river were gardens. During the dry seasons, the corn stalks would dry and wait for our bush-burning adventures. Before the bush-burning adventures, there was another kind of adventure. The stalk of the corn is strong and creates smoke when lit. They served as pretend cigarettes. It was a rite of passage that older boys would take younger boys behind the garden, where people do not pass, and introduce them to their first smoke and drink.

I was 11 years old when Muffy took me behind the garden. Muffy was a neighbor whose family had a television in the early 2000s. Of course, I liked him. I liked his whole family. Whether it was him I admired, or what his family had, I don't know, but I saw them as above us, and I idolized them for that. I listened and did everything he said. One evening, I was on my way to get water when I met him. He was also heading to the river. I tagged along. As we walked, other boys from the community joined us. When we approached the river, he declared that we should follow him. Soon, we were behind a garden, where no one respectable went. There were people, but not the kind of people you wanted your parents to see you with. And they were doing things we were sure would make our parents mad.

Muffy began by telling us that we were boys about to become men. "A real man is a man who can do hard things, a man who can stand on his own, a man who can defy all the rules and survive," he said. He brought out a cigarette and took a puff. He then proceeded to cut off the stalk of a corn plant. He broke it into many pieces and passed it around.

"Real men also smoke cigarettes. But before you get there, you begin small. This is your first step. A real man will take this and not feel anything," he said. He lit the stalk and said we could begin. We did, slowly. When I inhaled the first gulp, I started coughing immediately. Other boys were also coughing hard. The bigger boys started laughing at us. They vowed that none of us would leave until we finished our stalk. That's when I started crying.

They pointed at me, laughing. "He is a girl. Look at him. He couldn't even stand a single gulp." Someone added, "He lives in a house full of girls. Do you expect he would be different? Just a girl with a man's body." They kept laughing even as I and all the other boys struggled.

Eventually, the stalks burned beyond any use. Then Muffy began again. "I just want to help you all become men. I want you all to be strong. This is how you become strong. The pain is only for the first time. After that, you enjoy it. Tomorrow, come again. If you want to be girls, then you can avoid this place. But if you want to be real men, then come, and we will help you."

Not surprisingly, the next day, a few other boys and I went back there. Why? We wanted to be men. We didn't want to be girls. I didn't want to be called a girl. I didn't like the other boys to remind me that I grew up in a house with only girls, nor to look at me as a girl in a boy's body. I wanted to prove myself. We went the next day, and this time around, they treated us better. We finished our stalk without much choking. So, after all, they were right.

That day, they gave us a warning: we were not allowed to tell anyone that they were giving us anything. They said that this was men's talk and these were men's activities. If we told anyone, they would beat us. The warning registered. We didn't want to betray our initiation. We felt like a select group of boys receiving something unique. We would never tell anyone. Our peer group of initiation included Daniel, Stephen, and Henry. We returned there every day for a week and got prepared to smoke the real thing. I guess they didn't give us the real thing because the real thing cost money, and they didn't want to spare it for some group of boys who had nothing to offer them in return. After the first week, they told us that we were ready. They promised to give us the "real thing" the following week.

Fortunately for me, I left for secondary school at All Nations Academy, Bokkos, seventy-seven kilometers from Jos, by Saturday of that weekend. Unfortunately, Daniel, Stephen, and Henry went to day schools nearby. When I returned for a break, they were already good smokers. By the time I graduated from secondary school, they were all struggling with drug addiction. The only thing that separated me from them was that my family sent me kilometers away to school, where I couldn't complete the initiation process. My interest in drinking or smoking never developed again.

This was the beginning of my motion. Moving away from Jenta was the first step to a different life. Many friends who didn't have the opportunity to attend a school outside of Jenta went on a different path. Some have spent years in prison, others have become drug addicts, and some have died in the most unfortunate circumstances. Daniel has been to jail twice; Stephen struggles with drug addiction and became a father before he was twenty. In 2020, there was a big gunfight between two different gangs in Jenta. Henry was one of those killed. He had been a gang member for most of his adult life.

I escaped similar fates only because I was not around to participate.

CHAPTER 6

MOVING AWAY

After primary school, a reputable school only one transport drop away from my house, offered me a scholarship. I was excited about the scholarship endorsement. My parents were proud of me, and we looked forward to my starting school. There was just one thing left for me to provide before resuming my education: I was to undergo a medical checkup. While in the hospital undergoing the checkup, the man at the counter entered into a casual conversation with me. We chatted briefly, and then he asked Mother why we were in the hospital. She explained. He asked for my academic results, and she gave them to him. He glanced over the pages, shaking his head, and told her, "That's not the kind of school for your boy."

With that short sentence, he altered my life forever. That school was just one drop from Jenta, if I had attended there, it is almost certain that I would be visiting home, my connection with the bad influences in Jenta would have remained and probably ruined me. By going to a school far away from Jenta, it was certain that I could not connect with the bad influences there. That man, whose name I do not know even today, influenced my life in a way I could not understand. While I was building my case against God, He was putting in place angels in human form all around me guiding me to a better path.

That man suggested that Mother take me to a school in Bokkos called All Nations Academy. As though under some spell, my mother accepted the suggestion without question. Mother contacted Mr. Mathew Barde, a staff member of All Nations Academy. By Thursday of the following week, I was in Bokkos for another standard entrance examination and interview. One particular question I failed, which I will never forget, was to name the parts of speech. I tried several times but just didn't get it, I knew nothing about it because no one had taught me about it. After the interview, the teacher who conducted the process taught me about the parts of speech. It was a gentle reminder that there are things you will never know unless someone teaches you. Ultimately, I reached the required mark, and the school accepted me. By the next week, I had resumed school with incomplete supplies and clothing. My mother said she would bring the remainder on the school's visiting day.

The first Saturday at All Nations Academy is a day I will never forget. We were a bunch of boys seated on the bed, chatting about everything. It was our first weekend together. We were getting to know each other. That Saturday was our first full day when we didn't have to attend class or participate in any morning activity. Or so we thought. As we were seated on the bed chattering away, we heard a voice saying,

"Who are those? Come out here and kneel down."

We were startled. First, who was that? We soon learned it was "the" Mr. Aminu, a short, heavily muscled man who looked like a wrestler straight out of WWE. He was the games master (physical education teacher) known for being a no-nonsense teacher. He had a reputation, and on that Saturday, he was going to live up to it. We marched out trembling and knelt. That day, Mr. Aminu gave us ten lashes each on our buttocks. He caned nearly all the boys in that hostel on that day, and when he finished, he was walking tall. From that day on, I knew I needed to avoid this man. If he were going right, I'd make sure to go left.

Why did he flog us? Saturday was for inspection at All Nations Academy. Our crime on this day was chatting instead of preparing for the inspection, a weekly activity on Saturday mornings. It was a sacred activity, as important as breakfast or lunch. We were new, and no one had told us. But he didn't care. This was Boarding School 101. Ignorance of the law is not a defense against the consequences of breaking the law. You can't say, "I did not know." Just saying that was a crime. My buttocks hurt for many days, and I could hardly sit. It was the most painful lash I'd ever received, and it would not be the last. Over the next six years, I would receive many lashes for many things, both justified and unjustified, and some even more vicious, but I would never forget that first one. It was my baptism.

Welcome to boarding school, buddy.

From that day till the day I graduated, I hated inspection days.

Breaking the Rules

The boarding school was nothing like what I had imagined; not as bad as some described it to be, but not as good as I wanted it to be. In our final year of primary school, we heard many scary stories about boarding schools from relatives and family friends. For many of us, attending a boarding school was the last thing we wanted to do. But in my case, I had no choice. Mother was Supreme Leader. What she decreed stood like the pyramids of Giza, unshakable by any argument.

New students are assigned to senior students as school fathers, these seniors were to help the new students integrate into a boarding house. I was assigned to a fantastic senior student named Pannan. We were both in Green House, Room 12. Even though he was older, he was fully committed to my well-being and protection. While Pannan could fend off any bullying seniors who were his peers or younger, he was powerless against older seniors and teachers. I knew I could rely on him to handle those he could, but beyond that, I had to fend for myself. Faced with limited options, I had to choose: either follow the rules and mostly stay safe or break them and face constant punishment. I opted mostly to adhere to the rules. Mostly.

Avoiding punishment preoccupied my mind. But I would rather accept punishment than plead my way out of it. If I were to face the consequences, I would first want to enjoy the full fruits of my crime. For instance, if I were late for evening preps, I would choose to nap in the hostel instead of struggling to attend class. I would face punishment either way, so I chose to accept the punishment later. This way, I enjoyed some sleep, which any student would covet. When punishment came, I offered myself entirely to the altar for slaughter. This time, no voice would call on the senior to stop. The lash always came down.

In my junior year, there was a song that some seniors would make us sing before flogging us. The lyrics went something like this:

> *Every bum bum, every bum bum, must be tortured*
> *Every bum bum, every bum bum, must be tortured*

It was an adaption of a Christian song.

> *Every living soul, every living soul, praises the Lord*
> *Every living soul, every living soul, praises the Lord*

Religiosity

It is no surprise that we corrupted a Christian song for such a purpose. We had become numb to Christian things. The unceasing rituals at All Nations almost made me mad at God. Every day began with a meeting in the school compound, about five minutes from the hostel, starting with praise and worship songs, then devotional teaching, and then prayer. After the prayers, we returned to the hostel, did our morning duties, and headed to class. On some days, we would pray again before the classes commenced. Every evening, we held devotions in our hostels before sleep; another devotional teaching, more praise and worship songs, then prayers again. Before every meal, we had corporate prayers, and sometimes, some zealot would preach a sermon before anyone could eat a bite.

All Nations Academy was a religious institution. Every moment of our lives was centered around religious activities, seven days a week. Every student, regardless of their convictions, must perform all specified religious duties. While the meetings and rituals were well-intentioned, I chafed against such indoctrination. I wanted to be independent, to find my own way. It wasn't that I was against God; deep down, I desired to find God for myself. I wanted to love God, not just follow the rules. All my life, I had seen people follow this stern Law Giver by keeping the rules, but I hadn't seen evidence of any of love for Him. Maybe God loved us, but we didn't love Him. I wanted to love Him.

On Wednesdays, we had special mid-week prayers that lasted an hour after school hours. The worst thing about this Wednesday ritual was that it was also the day that we received the worst meal combination from breakfast to dinner. In the morning, we had pap, made of ground corn, which was different from the porridge and tea we had on other days. Pap makes you sleepy. In the afternoon, we had tasteless rice made with groundnut oil, and in the evening, we had tuwo—the ever-present tuwo—with either dry okra or our least favorite *kukah* soup (Kukah was hated because it required patience to make it properly, something that was rarely present in a boarding school kitchen.) Honestly, there was nothing to look forward to on Wednesdays.

Then Sunday came, as it always did. Supposedly it was a day of rest, but according to whom? Morning devotions, breakfast, morning service from 8 am to 11 am, Bible studies, lunch by 1 pm, and evening service made Sundays exhausting. We were getting heavy doses of religious indoctrination, and we had no say.

The last Friday of every month was fasting and night vigil. It was these Fridays that made me miss my mother all the more. Mother was deeply religious, but she would never force us to fast. I couldn't believe I could find myself in a situation that would make my mother look liberal. We would fast from morning till afternoon. We would attend regular classes, prayer sessions, and other school activities while fasting. This was almost a punishment for growing and ravenous students between twelve and eighteen. After breaking our fast at about 2 pm, we would rest a bit and then get involved in intensive school cleanup that often included cutting the grass, repainting chalkboards, etc. By 10 pm that same Friday, we would return for a night vigil until 3 am or 4 am. Guess what time we would rise? 7 am.

Boarding school was a drill; to me, it seemed like a brutal military drill. Looking back now, I understand why they did what they did, and their intentions were genuine. There is no better way to impress something upon a child than through rituals. But for a boy with a mind like mine, who questions everything, it was tough to survive. I couldn't express my opinion, so I expressed it through rebellion. I found many ways to push the limits of the system. Thankfully, it was only me and a few others. The system survived and did its job remarkably, producing many fine men and women.

Scenes Against the System

Rather than the system breaking, it nearly broke me. I was clever and did many things purely to test the system. Was it as solid as it claimed to be? Was it good? Here is the good news: a good system will always beat a clever person. In retrospect, I am glad I lost.

One way I fought the system was in food rations. Every student was entitled to a single dish. There was a popular line in school: "One man, one dish." To me, those were just words. I always attempted to get two dishes. But as my reputation increased within the school and my face became more familiar, I realized I had to stop. I did.

At the same time, there was another student named Alhamdu Abbe. Our first names rhymed, "AlhamdU," and "LengdUng." People often said we looked alike based on our facial expressions and were also similar in height. However, that's where the similarities ended. Alhamdu was more of a criminal than I was. He would commit the crime, and when the authorities saw me, they would swear it was me. On many occasions, I had to argue hard to prove my innocence. At some point, I just decided to find out who this guy was and to know him. Eventually, we became friends, which made our situation worse. Now, we were committing the crimes together, a combination of two juvenile minds with no regard for authority and no fear of punishment. To this day, we have remained friends. He is one person I can call any day in times of need. What else can bond people more than shared experiences of crime and punishment?

In the early days of school, when there was still no class prefect, every teacher had his favorite pupil. This busybody would find the teacher in the staff room to remind him of class times, collect student assignments, and report on class activities. Most students coveted attention and did more than necessary to please the teachers.

One of these teacher's pets was a girl I admired in my class. Her name was Janet. But the admiration was not reciprocal. When I realized this, I decided to fight back by saying embarrassing things about her. But she turned out to be even more Machiavellian than I was. She began writing my name on the list of noise makers. Each day, she would write my name first. Her argument was always that I would be on the list either way, so she might as well write it. On the other hand, sometimes I would stand up, go to her, and tell her, "Hope my name is not on the list?" Well, that was one sure way to get my name on the list. Other times, I would publicly announce in the class that I am quiet, as everyone can see. That, too, got my name on the list. I was establishing the crime. Usually, she would write "x2" if I spoke more than once, and she multiplied it each time I made more noise.

One day, I got pissed off by the whole trap and decided I might as well enjoy myself and make the noise so I could deserve the punishment. My name had "x30" next to it. My other friend, Nandom, had x50. Usually, the teachers who came to punish noisemakers did not take the x2 or x30 written in front of their names seriously. Everyone got the same punishment. But on this particular day, the teacher was new, and she took the x30 literally. When she finished whooping us, our arms were red. My hands were swollen for days. What little admiration I had for Janet turned into hate.

Typically, truant students and those with the lowest grades were seated at the back of the class. I did not have bad grades but still hated the front seats. Throughout my stay in school, I strove to sit at the back of the class. The back seat allowed one to avoid being noticed by teachers, which meant that one could do other things while the rest of the class was deeply engrossed in learning. In my case, I used the back seat to read stories and write letters.

At first, teachers would see me caught in some school rule violation with other students and express surprise, saying, "Even you? What are you doing with this caliber of people? I expected so much more from you." But the more they said that the more I hated their corrections. I didn't want anyone to have expectations of me. I wanted to live on my own. I wanted my freedom to do anything, including the freedom to be wrong. (This is a behavior I noticed with many kids from the ghetto like me; we just didn't care about our actions and consequences. We believed our birthplace determined our futures, so we did not believe our actions could alter our lives for good or bad. For ghetto kids, it was "YOLO," You Only Live Once. We only get one chance to have fun, so we would break the rules and damn the consequences. No matter what, in the end, we would choose fun.)

We had a strict physics teacher who lived by the rules and forced everyone to do the same. Mr. John gave detailed instructions. Do A, B, and C at this time, that time, and that time. Everything was supposed to be by the book. He lived by the book, so why couldn't we? If we deviated, he would punish us severely. I didn't get along well with Mr. John, as I couldn't live by the book. I questioned the rules, and we clashed often. But due to the power dynamics of our tit-for-tat, he always won. For a long time, I searched for a way to get back at him. Then I found one.

Once you figure out the formula for people who strictly adhere to rules, you can easily crack it. The only way I could get back at Mr. John was through exams. He had a reputation for being a teacher who was stingy with grades. His best students often came out with only a B. When we resumed that term, I discovered that Mr. John always gave his essay questions from the previous years of our WASSCE (West African Senior School Certificate Examination). So, from the beginning of the term, I studied all the past questions for the last twenty years. I solved them and ensured I knew them like the back of my hand. Exams came and went. Before distributing the marked scripts, Mr. John made a short speech.

"Your scripts are here. There is one particular student whose scripts I had to mark three times. The first time I marked, he scored 39/40 in the essay. The second time he scored 40/40. I had to mark again to ensure I did the right thing. Now, I am here to ask you all. Did any of you see Lengdung Apolos cheat during the exams?".

There was silence. He added a few more words to encourage the class to speak up. No one spoke up. And so he gave the scripts to the class.

That term, I had done everything to get that grade. I'd studied and prepared for every possible question by dotting the Is and crossing the Ts. I had won in my own way. Nothing pisses off a disciplinarian more than seeing an undisciplined person on whom he has given up surpassing his most crucial standard.

I Renounced Violence

As a kid, I was lanky. It seemed as though a strong wind could throw me down. The physical frailty from my birth followed me to childhood and into adulthood. My mother would often warn me that I was a slim boy and, therefore, I should avoid any fights with anyone in the community, especially a group of boys called The Babas. The Babas got their name from their dad, whose nickname was Baba. They were short, well-built laborers. Their dad was a mason and often took his boys along to help him. Mother said, "Those boys are beyond you, they will beat you one day." But I couldn't avoid them because they were one of the best groups to play with, as they could often get you out of trouble. Mother's logic was that they could beat you someday; my logic was that they could save me from other fights in the community. My logic prevailed time and time again, until one day when it failed.

That day, I had offended Aya, the youngest of them. In anger and argument, I threw away his food. For the Babas, one thing mattered above all else: food. Food was supreme; they had to eat and didn't always know where the next meal would come from. Their father's mason work was job-to-job, and on some days, there was no work. No work meant there was no money for food that day. Through experience, they learned to cherish and eat every bit of every meal that came their way. I had poured out his food, perhaps the only meal he would have that day. He attacked me instantly, and we got into a fight. A fight? That was no fight. It was a beating. He beat me black and blue. He only stopped because his brothers intervened and said that the beating had gone far enough. They said he would have killed me.

Since that day, I renounced violence. I am a firm believer in non-violence. Folks, let us learn to resolve our differences with words only.

This resolve was not some great moral triumph. I renounced violence not because I came to a profound spiritual truth like Mahatma

Gandhi or Martin Luther King, Jr. but because I accepted the reality that I was a skinny kid who had no chance in physical combat. I could not live by the sword, because the sword didn't choose me to wield it.

After I renounced violence, I had to develop another tool to fight back. My words became my weapon. My mouth could deliver blows even if I couldn't gain victory with my hands. Better still, with my words I could cause harm that would last longer than cuts and bruises. I found that others picked up the clever insults I used on people, and they stuck for a long time. As I did this, my word game also improved significantly.

Our classmate in ANA, Rita Malan, was a dark, beautiful girl who was gentle and quiet. My friend Nandom and I took advantage of her meekness. Each time she walked into the class, we would stand by the door and say, "Here comes the most beautiful girl in the world. Her cousins are in the jungle, and she is here." We had just been taught the theory of evolution in class, and we learned that humans evolved from monkeys. Everyone would burst out laughing. One day, she was walking in when I stood up and started mimicking a monkey, and we went on to say more hurtful words. She broke down and cried. That day, a senior student, Peace Agowa, was passing by when she saw her crying. When she learned what had happened, she flogged us till our arms swelled.

My wordsmithing found other outlets—letter writing. I would write letters for seniors and mates to their prospective girlfriends. I would often do a trade for the letter. I would agree to write a pleasant letter for a senior, and he would agree to protect me against his mates who wanted to beat me. I always did my best with this as the safety of my buttocks depended on it. Sometimes, I would enter into a long-term contract with the senior. I would handle all his correspondence with his girlfriend, and he would be my protector for the whole session. This agreement worked well even after the romantic episode passed. The senior continued to protect me to avoid the crushing embarrassment he would have to endure if she found out that all his love letters, which were wordy and sweet, were written by me.

To boost my writing enterprise, I bought a book of letters each time I came to school. To get to Bokkos, a one-hour drive from home, I had to get to the transportation park and wait for some hours for the car to fill with passengers before it would leave. Father was against late traveling, so I always arrived at the park very early. Arriving at 7 am on some days, the cars would not leave till 2 pm when people returned from church. During those seven hours, I would wander around the park, looking to buy books from the book vendors. I would pick a short one on text messages to friends, families, and lovers. I would add story books like "The Tortoise and the Hare." The books of letters were the wells I drank from as I poured forth the letters I wrote.

The books I bought were valuable in other ways. I would read them to fill up my knowledge bank, and immediately after reading them, I would sell them to my classmates. At first, I brought the books I had purchased to school and read them, but by the third week of resumption, they were all borrowed and never returned. Next session, I changed my tactics. I decided to read them carefully, preserve them in good shape, and sell them. Often, I would purchase ten books for 150 Naira per copy. I read them all within the first week of classes, and by the second week, I was marketing my merchandise. I sold them for 200 or 300 Naira each, a nice profit.

Loopholes

Every offense at All Nations Academy resulted in punishment. School rules were strict. If you arrived late for dinner, you would be punished before being served; in some cases, you would even be denied the meal. If you arrived late for class, you would be punished. If you arrived late for games, you would be punished. The worst crime of all was to arrive late for Sunday service. You would be punished severely before going into the hall to receive the mercy of God.

I was found guilty of all these offenses in my first few weeks. This daily life of offense and punishment was not sustainable. I had to find another way to live. Yet I was convinced I could not live obediently and keep the rules. I wanted a loophole.

And I found one.

A senior sent me to the hostel to wash his uniforms. I could not complete the task on time, so I arrived late. When the senior on duty stopped me among those who were late, I told him, "Senior Pannan asked me to wash his uniform. That's why I am late."

"You can pass."

Just like that? Huh? That was the loophole I needed. The next time I was late for a function, I told the senior on duty a staff member had sent me. When the staff on duty stopped me, I told him the Vice Principal, who was my distant uncle, had sent me. My logic was that those on duty would never ask their superiors whether or not they sent me, as that would disrespect their authority. It worked every time. Eventually, I took my deception to the highest level and would tell the staff on duty, "The principal sent me." They never confirmed, never checked, and I survived.

My success in this also increased my boldness. My friends, who noticed that I often got away with the same crimes they had committed, began to ask me what I used that helped me get away. I told them, "It is all about guts, and in my family, we have a lot of it. Sorry, you are not in my family." But on some days, I would pity my favorite friends and co-opt them into the escape plan.

These were the basic realities students at All Nations Academy faced. I got bored of these schemes and followed a Lengdungian path, a path that would put me in more trouble than I imagined.

The Great Ones

The ultimate expression of my rebelliousness came forth in my SSS1 year through a group known as The Great Ones. The Great Ones consisted of five guys united in a common devotion to food. Our group name may have sounded like a terror group or a criminal gang, but our existential purpose was to eat as much food as possible. That's all we wanted. We lived to eat. Forget about the philosophical question of whether we live to eat or eat to live. At that time, if you'd put the question forward, we would have debated you and won.

I know a person didn't attend a boarding school if I hear them say they can't eat food at certain times of the night. Anyone who has a preference for a time of day they like to eat didn't attend a boarding school. We would be ready to eat if you woke us up at midnight. If you woke us up at 1 am, we would be ready to eat. If you woke us up at 6 am, we would be ready to eat. We were always ready to eat. Food dominated our thoughts, dominated our actions, and dominated our lives. If we missed a meal for some reason, it was like a near-death experience.

We would do all we could to get more than our share, including stealing food. But you see, we were principled; we would never steal from students. We always stole from the kitchen and only when we went to get our regular share.

Like most Nigerian boarding schools at the time, we did not have a cafeteria to eat our meals. Instead, the kitchen would serve our portion in an insulated food flask that we would take back to our rooms and eat while sitting on our beds. This arrangement made it difficult for people to notice our schemes.

We would collect more than one man's share by lying or returning more than once, which was easy to organize, at least for us. We didn't have to worry about other students reporting us, for the mere presence of food for secondary school students was the best distraction. Food was served according to the classes; JSS1 goes in first, JSS2, and then

JSS3. When we formed The Great Ones, we were in SSS1. We would go in just as JSS3 was rounding up and get our first share. Then, we'd wait until SSS2 was going in to get our second share. Sometimes, we would even get a third share. It all depended on which staff member was on duty, which student served the food, and how loud we were during our entrance.

The Great Ones gained their reputation by openly boasting about our feats. We would tell anyone willing to listen that we could return with another full food flask, and we almost always succeeded. People were amazed and couldn't understand how we kept succeeding against the odds. Perhaps the fact that most people thought it was impossible contributed to our success. Even the authorities believed it was impossible, so they didn't bother with stringent measures. On the few occasions when they caught us, we swore on heaven and earth that we hadn't received our share. Our bold confidence and persistent denials often convinced them. In a profoundly religious school, just saying "I swear" could sway the listener. Damn the consequences of breaking the Ninth Commandment, we didn't care much about religion at that time. For us, it was just part of the atmosphere.

Another area in which I excelled—besides securing the next meal— was sports. Everyone wanted to have me on their team. I was lanky but creative and fast, and I knew how to put my opponents to shame. Football was another avenue through which I took my revenge on the teachers and seniors. I would dribble around them and embarrass them so much that some would harm me intentionally.

One episode related to football that I will never forget was an inter-house competition when I was in JSS3. The inter-house competition had begun, and our house, the Green, had played and qualified for the finals. During the tournament, I played an essential role in helping my team reach that point. The organizers scheduled the finals for a big day and invited several outsiders, parents, the PTA, community leaders, and some bigshots in Bokkos. Some days before the final, a serious problem arose. Dad had not paid the fees for that term. I didn't blame him. He was doing his best. As was the school's policy, if you were behind on school fees, you were sent home. Before leaving, several of my housemates came to remind me of the finals and to get my assurance that I would be back in time. It was almost a week away. I felt I could make it no matter what. In my mind, I would return to school by Monday at the latest. That was the longest it had ever taken my parents to resolve any school fee issue.

I got home and cheerfully reported to my dad. For students, going home was always a delightful, unexpected break. Of course, he wasn't as happy as I was—for he knew the financial situation. I did not foresee that I would not be back in school by Monday, not on Tuesday, Wednesday, Thursday, or Friday. And when Game Day came on Saturday, I was still at home.

That night was one of the longest nights of my life. Everything reminded me that I was supposed to be in school, playing in the finals. I couldn't get it out of my head. As evening came and passed, I imagined so many scenarios. I imagined that we would win. I imagined that we won the football game and other trophies, too. I imagined that we trashed our opponent ten goals to nothing. I was an optimistic person.

I returned to school the following Monday, and the first person who welcomed me told me I was a coward, that I betrayed them and made them losers. The final match reached extra time, and there was no winner after extra time. So it went into penalties. The Green House lost after a player who was a defender, someone not supposed to take a penalty kick, took the shot and lost. It was my penalty kick he took.

Everyone told me how I could have been a game-changer. It was especially painful because I couldn't explain the real reason to my teammates. I could not tell them my dad hadn't paid my school fees. I was ashamed of our poverty.

This experience entered my growing catalog of what poverty could do to a person. I hated poverty all the more.

Bush attack

Pit latrines were the toilets that we could use to answer the call of nature at All Nations Academy. They were smelly and unkempt. Around the school were thickets next to farmlands. During the farming season, the bushes in the thickets could grow taller than the average student. Senior students tired of the pit latrines would venture into these bushes to defecate. We renamed the call of nature a "bush attack." You could hear students saying, "I am going for a bush attack. Are you going along?"

Attacking the bush was not just about answering the call of nature. It was also about stealing farm produce like potatoes, fresh pepper, carrots, green beans, and cabbage. I hated bush attack in the sense of answering the call of nature, but I loved bush attack in terms of the items I could return to the hostels with. In those days, we used this to get back at teachers we believed were mean to us. Nearly all of the teachers who lived on the campus had farms nearby. I had a principle that I would never steal from the farm of a person I didn't know. But I had no mercy for teachers I had perceived as being cruel. I would harvest as though I was a shareholder in the farm. Mostly, this small harvest made no difference to the farmer, but as a student, it made a lot of difference to me. It made me money.

I had a big garment called *babban riga,* which translates to big cloth or gown in Hausa. Men in northern Nigeria usually wear it. I used it for drama presentations. I converted it to my harvest clothing. At night, I would stroll down the farm, harvest the produce, and use the babban riga as my cover. One day, I realized that using a babban riga made the expeditions repetitious because I could hold only as much as my hands could carry. I had to do this every night to gather the garnishment for the next day. I decided to use a bucket and the babban riga was ample enough to cover the bucket.

When I returned to the hostel at night, my produce would fill a twelve inch by six inch school box and last more than two days. But by that time, the signs of spoilage were becoming evident. I started selling it off, and my new enterprise was born. I would no longer harvest for myself; I would harvest and sell to other students. Some students were curious enough to ask where I got the produce, so I told them I bought it in town. This answer was not satisfactory, and they had suspicions about it. They could have reported me, but they couldn't prove the exact place I was getting it from. I never revealed my business secret to anyone. The more I harvested, the more money I made, and the more comfortable in school I became. But as I was doing all this, I was missing evening preps.

Preps were the most convenient time for me to do my harvesting operation. I missed more preps than ever before. Some seniors began to notice my absence in preps and would often search for me afterward. I learned the art of appearing for reading-time for twenty minutes and then disappearing for the remaining two hours. Twenty minutes was enough to show myself to some serious people and sometimes even the senior on duty, and then I would disappear. The next time someone came to accuse me of being absent for preps, I would deny it vehemently, saying, "I was at preps, I even came early. I stayed in the JSS2B classroom to read. I didn't want to read in my classroom as I would be disturbed. I also met senior James. If you don't believe me, ask senior James".

And they would ask the senior if he saw me.

"Senior James, did you see Lengdung during preps?"

"Yes, yes, I did. He was in JSS2B."

While I escaped all the human snares that could nab me, there was one I couldn't escape, and it came at the end of the term—my report card. My poor grades revealed my absences. My GPA went down for the first time in my secondary school days. It wasn't bad; in fact, I was still one of the best in the class. But it was below my previous performance. Absence in preps had taken its toll in the one area I couldn't change. Consequences always follow actions, no matter how one tries to avoid them.

To make matters worse, this session would determine our prefect-ship. A lackluster performance would deny me the highest prefectship role. Only the brightest boy and girl in the class could receive that distinction. But I was still lucky. The selection of the senior prefect primarily depended on the highest performance; hardly any other factor mattered. If reputation or staying out of trouble had mattered, I wouldn't have been in the race. Although my performance was not my best, all those ahead of me were girls. Yes, I wasn't at the top of the class, but I was still at the top of the boys.

My academic performance was my refuge each time life was falling apart for me. It was the one thing I always had going; many people had told me I was intelligent, and I never doubted it. With the stellar results every three months, there was no reason to doubt it. My confidence that I could hold my own in any academic environment with any kid helped me stay above the prejudices I faced and the bad decisions I made. It also opened doors for me to opportunities I would not have gotten in any other way.

BLESSINGS FROM ALL NATIONS ACADEMY

As a result of my many rebel escapades, I became a magnet to rebels, outliers, and outcasts. In JSS2, the school assigned three new students to my room. These outcasts were no ordinary students. They were the most unlikely for such a school as ours. They were Muslims. For a Christian school, nothing could be more contrarian. They were enrolled in the school because their fathers believed that missionary education, which was how Western education arrived in Nigeria, would benefit their boys. When they arrived, they were objects of curiosity. They were allowed to practice their religion but must additionally attend all Christian religious activities: prayers, Bible study, mid-week service, night vigils, etc. One of the things that became popular with their arrival was that everyone who considered himself a serious Christian was competing to be known as the person who converted these Muslim boys. These devoted Christians constantly bombarded them.

During those early days, the one thing I never raised with them was the subject of religion. That made them very open to me, and our friendship blossomed. I realized that they wanted friendship more than they wanted my religion. Early on, I accepted them for their faith and stopped trying to convert them. They stayed at All Nations Academy for six years, and when they finished, none of them converted to Christianity. It was fortunate that I accepted this reality early. It saved me from heartbreak and gave me a wonderful friendship that continues to bless me to this day. Even while at ANA, the friendships blessed me.

Sallah often occurred in the middle of the school session. They began with a thirty-day fasting. I would frequently shield them from work, provide them basic things such as water for ablution, or just some safety from seniors whenever they didn't want to engage in a school activity. After the thirty-day fast, they would return home for a week to celebrate the main event. When they returned, they always came with a lot of goodies. For us students, their return was often like a visit from parents. They always brought us snacks, meat, *chin chin* (a crunchy, sweet, and spicy fried dough snack), and other provisions. I cherished these gifts. Perhaps they helped to seal our friendship all the more.

Of these friends, the one whose life has blessed me the most and with whom I've interacted the most is Abdulrasheed. One time, we had an intense argument about Islam and Christianity; it was a grand debate that made us miss our dinner and brought a significant number of students to listen to us. There was no winner, but there was more understanding. It was the first time I became curious about Islam, and I asked Abdul to bring a Quran for me when next he was resuming school. He never brought one. It was many years later that I learned that the Quran is so precious to Muslims that it is not given to an 'infidel'—quite a contrast with the Bible, which is freely given to anyone and everyone.

Although I did not get a Quran from Abdul, our friendship survived beyond All Nations Academy and continues to this day. It is an irony that it was in a Christian school that I met a Muslim friend that would help me understand Islam and the reality of living with someone of a fundamentally different worldview.

An Overflowing Earth

There were moments of fun at ANA, moments that became shared memories for the students and that we continue to laugh about whenever two or three ANA old students are gathered. One of those moments involved a boy called Andy Dayak.

Andy Dayak was an eccentric student whose life was devoted to the noble pursuits of making people laugh and eating food. Once, the school football team traveled to Mangu Local Government Area for a match, and the kitchen staff preserved their food in a pot. Andy sneaked into the kitchen and started eating directly from the pot. Unfortunately for him, a staff member walked into the kitchen as he ate. Instead of running away, Andy jumped into the giant pot. The teacher caught him soaked in the mess he had created. Andy was flogged and then paraded around the school as the "pot criminal."

But Andy was also a gifted student whose moments of brilliance showed up unexpectedly. One day, the geography teacher, Mr. Maxwell Ajogor, was teaching about the earth and its surface. He said, "Seventy percent of the earth is covered with water..." In a previous class, he had taught that the earth is spherical. Andy raised his hand, saying he had a question. Mr. Maxwell Ajogor granted him the opportunity.

"Sir, you had said the earth is spherical in the previous class?"

"Yes, that's correct."

"And now you say that 70% of the earth is water. If that is so, why isn't the water pouring?"

"You foolish boy, how can the water pour?" Mr. Maxwell responded.

The whole class burst out laughing. The question was funny, childish, but also smart. But we couldn't see it at the time. The truth is, none of us understood the mechanism behind all of it. But, unlike Andy, we were too proud to appear ignorant.

As I grew older, I realized that's how most people behave. They would rather pretend to know than display ignorance and receive wisdom. I could not shake this thought.

All Nations Academy was many things to me. It was the place where I became conscious of everything. There, I learned to appreciate the differences in people and the differences in how Christians practice their faith. I learned to survive. Although we had teachers who were very involved in our lives, I was still on my own. A boarding school forces a child to weather the world independently. I learned critical life skills. Above all, the lesson that would remain with me for the rest of my life is that people will always hold an opinion about me. Whether or not that opinion is correct, they will always judge me by that. A quote I once found has stuck with me: "There is only one way to avoid criticism: do nothing, say nothing, and be nothing."

But I didn't plan to do, say, or be nothing.

I was tall, at the top of my class, had excellent football skills, and was a highly sought-after school debater. I hung out with the coolest kids in class and held an opinion about everything. No one could accuse me of indifference. I was radical. I was unrefined, enjoyed humiliating others, and much more; I was as selfish as you could imagine.

When I introduced myself as a boy from Jenta, my identity was sealed. There had been a few other boys from Jenta at that point. Timothy Eneche, Joel Kuzayet, Longji Dabit, and Peter Kurdor. Of the four, only Peter Kurdor was tolerable, and only because of his academic performance. Timothy Eneche was among the first students flogged on the Assembly ground in All Nations Academy. Joel Kuzayet was notorious for missing preps, and Longji Dabit was known for being late to school. The Jenta boys' were no company of the good guys. The assumption was that I was just like them. It was not far from the truth. I went on to live up to the image.

It was no surprise, therefore, that I had strong critics. I had a choice; those criticisms could crush me, or they could make me. They made me, hardened me. I learned the art of examining an argument, recognizing the faults, and dumping the irrelevant parts. It was at All Nations Academy that I learned to debate. I would take an extreme view for the sake of argument, merely to turn those around me into debate opponents. These were only lessons I learned at the end of my journey in All Nations Academy, after making mistakes that almost got me expelled from school.

The judgments others made about me were true; I was nothing to be proud of. I was not proud of myself. This realization was a significant mental shift. It meant I knew something had to change. The change came gradually, beginning right there at All Nations Academy. In many ways, I cannot imagine how my life would have turned out if I had attended any other school. In retrospect, the disciplined religious environment that All Nations Academy gave me a glimpse of what a religious worldview could be like.

But you see, All Nations Academy was important not only because of the things I did while there but also because of what it did to me. I wasn't the only one taking action. The ANA environment was acting on me. You can see this in what happened between my arrival and my exit. An encounter with a particular teacher signified the long journey I took at All Nations Academy.

Teacher of the Year

The first class I attended at All Nations Academy was an English class taught by Mr. Augustine Ambok. He asked us to read a passage from our English textbook. Like most people in the class, I was rushing, too eager to read to show my skill. I started reading, and he stopped me within a few seconds, saying, "Hey, my friend. Don't be stupid. Is that how you read? You don't know how to read. I wonder how you are going to survive."

Although I was reading the book, I wasn't reading at all. I was only saying the words, and I was saying them too fast to convey any meaning.

As you can imagine, I was embarrassed. Under the scrutiny of Mr. Ambok, I survived long enough that in my final year, I was given the Best Student in English award by the same teacher while I presented the Best Teacher of the Year award to him. All Nations Academy was that sort of academic environment—a challenging but supportive place where all teachers were deeply committed to our intellectual progress.

Mr. Ambok also played a role in making me fall in love with literature. In SSS1, students had to choose classes aligned with their chosen areas of study. Science classes were for science students, humanities classes were for humanities students, and social science classes were for social science students. If you chose to focus on science, you couldn't study subjects such as literature and commerce. I chose the sciences. However, because our classes were joined without a ceiling, I could hear some of the teachings from a humanities class. Mr. Ambok had a loud voice, and literature was a subject that required a lot of reading, so I followed many of his literature classes. He would come into class, write the topic on the board, and announce it loudly, asking the students to repeat it after him. As he was doing this in his class, I was taking notes in my class over the wall, sometimes to the detriment of whatever subject I was supposed to be studying.

After school, I would rush to my humanities friends and borrow their literature textbooks. During this process, I was introduced to *So Long: A Letter* by Mariama Ba, *Ambassadors of Poverty* by P.O.C Umeh, and *Othello* by William Shakespeare. This appreciation for the humanities, while I was in the sciences, was an early indication of a life principle I've held onto: the best way to live is to enjoy the cross-pollination of the humanities and the sciences. To me, the division of careers into specializations of specific fields is one of the errors of modern man. One can enjoy the humanities and still be a scientist. I've tried to live that way, at least.

Mr. Ambok was a unique teacher who put emotion into whatever he was reading. Although I could not see him do this, I could hear it from my class and imagine him. His ability to captivate students with this teaching style made students nickname him "Mr. Polite," a name he hated. But when teenagers give you a name, and they realize you hate it, it makes them use it all the more. The name stuck.

There was only one subject that I never did well in—the Hausa language. The Nigerian curriculum requires students to take one language class. Hausa is a common language spoken in Jos. It is both a language and a tribal group. One would expect that due to my upbringing, Hausa would be easy. Wrong. I failed Hausa repeatedly. While I gained A's in other subjects, my only aspiration in Hausa was just a P for Pass. What made this painful was that I had a Hausa teacher who took a liking to me. Each failure was a disappointment to him and a strain on our friendship. My grades in Hausa did not improve, but our friendship survived the years.

I was the best student in my graduating class. I received many awards, and according to listeners, I delivered an inspiring speech. But the noblest thing I did was to present the Best Teacher Award to Mr. Augustine Ambok, our English teacher. Mr. Ambok represented the cadre of teachers we had at All Nations Academy. They were dedicated to their work, intelligent, and eager to squeeze the best juice out of us.

My favorite teacher was Mr. Chinnan. He taught Agricultural Science. He was not my favorite teacher because of Agricultural Science. He was my favorite teacher because of what he did outside the classroom. Mr. Chinnan had a talent for befriending rebellious boys and girls. His favorite students were often the outliers, the outcasts and the rejected stones. He invaded our lives, spoke to us like a friend and warned us like a father. He provided what every rebellious child sought—to be understood! He understood me at a level that I did not understand myself. He possessed a rare gift: the ability to step into a student's inner world, where he'd walk alongside their thoughts, guiding and understanding. Mr. Chinnan was unique in that he was interested in why a person did a particular act. More than anyone, Mr.

Chinnan would be the guide who would inspire me in moments of despair, guide me in moments of confusion and point me to the fact that I can be something more than just rebellious.

Many teachers want to determine the course of their students' lives. Mr. Chinnan wanted his students to discover their course and chart it by themselves. He saw his role as that of a fellow traveler, not as a pointer. And because he was not as religious as the school, I valued his words all the more. What he said came from his heart and not from a religious program.

My academic performance was the major bright spot in my life. Come what may, I always did well in class. It helped to provide a cover for my other activities, so much that when I was punished, it was out of pity rather than vindictiveness. "How can a bright boy like you be involved in such an act?" my teachers always asked. They did not know then, nor did I realize it then, that my life up to that point was a reaction against the world. I had received negative reactions whenever I introduced myself as a boy from Jenta. I had received discrimination from the NGO when I was denied the chance to be a Governor because I was from Jenta. Teachers and students had condemned me for simply being from Jenta. I felt that the world was against me and I intended to fight back in the way that I could.

This contradiction of brilliance and indifference would collide in one circumstance that became the troubled hallmark of my secondary school days.

CHAPTER 8

PRESIDENT LENGDUNG

During my time at All Nations Academy, I joined Press Club, a student-led organization that taught skills about the broadcasting profession and kept our school community informed. Every Monday and Friday, we published news updates, sharing stories and highlights from around the campus and outside the campus. In SSS2, I became the president of the press club after an election that was a no-contest. The candidacy application was available for weeks, but I wasn't interested. Many Press Club members sent messages appealing to me to run for office as they felt I could play an essential role in improving it. I didn't consider the offer for two reasons. One, I was too absorbed in my school fees problems to consider other things. Second, I hated that students were already drawing parallels between my life and Peter Kurdor, my predecessor. He had been the senior prefect of the school and the president of Press Club. He was a tall, skinny youth from Jenta, and the school's foremost debater. A year ahead of me, he was about to graduate, and students and staff were comparing his scores and mine. I hated it, for although we were similar in all these respects, people compared us to shame me for my notorious behavior. I was tired of hearing, "Why can't you be more like Peter Kurdor?" At that point, I was already the senior prefect and the school's foremost debater. And, of course, I was from Jenta. So, I told myself I wouldn't throw my hat in the fight as I didn't want any more comparisons. However, as the deadline for the candidacy application approached, I began to change my mind. One evening, a few days before the close, I declared my intention to run and got the form. I started campaigning immediately. I was a fluent speaker, and supporters already wanted me to contest. When election day came, it was a landslide. Afterward, I made a good political move that surprised even me. The president was free to nominate anyone for a vacant role, so I nominated my competitor as vice president. It was the best decision I made as the new president of the press club. It was also a decision that would haunt me some months later.

My restless nature flowed into the press club, and as president, I initiated some reforms that reshaped it. One initiative we launched was new to the school. It was the suggestion box. Even then, I firmly believed in holding people to account. One way to do that was to ensure the anonymity of the reporter. Through the suggestion box, the press club introduced the school's first form of student empowerment. We designed a box with a lock and key. I had one key, and the principal had another. Anyone who had thoughts could write and place them in the suggestion box. The principal or I would look into the box every evening to remove the messages. It turned out that reading the messages became a novelty for the principal, Mr. Adisa. He was an exceptionally kind man who lent a listening ear to everyone. One day, he called on me to tell me that reading the letters was a delight, and he loved the initiative. Of course, I was proud.

The suggestion box led to students opening up on issues they could not open up about previously. Many messages expressed personal grievances; others offered suggestions that could not be implemented in the short run, and a few directly reported actions by seniors. Bullying was common; however, punishing a bully was not common, as reporting the act was a tricky thing. If a junior reported a senior, the senior might get penalized. Later on, the friends of the senior would punish the junior because reporting had to occur in the presence of the senior. The suggestion box changed this. A junior could privately report a senior and credibly deny reporting. This system did not eliminate bullying immediately, but it signaled to seniors that a new tool could be used against them, and it signaled to juniors that they had a new power.

One morning, I walked up to the suggestion box and saw it soaked with water. Most likely, an angry senior student did it. But who can stop an idea whose time has come? Watching the suggestion box became one of the duties of the campus security men.

Also, as president of the press club, I made another daring move, but this one could cost me my prefectship. We had two general assemblies every week, on Mondays and Fridays. Press Club had the opportunity to present news and an advert during the assemblies. Every Sunday and Thursday evening, two fast writers would go to the house of a staff member, mostly the principal, and watch the news, then write it into a news article that could be read the next day. The whole process was demanding and nearly impossible for most students. First, you would need a fast writer who could take down the headlines and some significant events, and then the person had to be creative enough to make it into a full news story that was interesting for young adults. The television carried the news from 7 pm to 8 pm or 9 pm to 10 pm. Also, the boys' hostel was quite a distance from the Principal's house. Hence, processing the news immediately after collection from the principal's house was impossible.

The process of turning the notes into news took a lot of time. Because we were writing on paper, one needed to recopy everything in his or her handwriting after he had received it to avoid problems with reading the next day. The complex procedure made it difficult to have different people doing different things. As a result, it was natural that a few people dominated the press club. The same faces recorded the news, rewrote it, and presented it the next day. A handful of students from the whole group were doing the work, and they were the ones improving. The remaining students who had joined the press club hoping to learn new skills and develop confidence were not learning anything as there was no opportunity for them.

I wanted to change this process.

There was only one solution: we had to find a way to get news at our own pace. Using a newspaper would have helped, but newspapers were unavailable in Bokkos then. I determined that the next best thing would be to get a phone. We had used this before whenever an old student visited or our teachers allowed us to use their phones, but it was very rare, and students having phones in school was illegal. So, what to do? I came up with a solution that would get me in trouble.

One of the reforms I made was that every news day would have a new broadcaster, and the people who would write the news had to be different from those who would cast it. We also strengthened the advertising arm of the press club. Previously, we only read adverts for things like exams, Sunday service, or generic adverts with moral lessons such as obedience, honesty, and discipline. Now we introduced a new kind of advert that involved the businesses around the school. Several staff members had businesses they were running. We went to them and told them we had an advert coming up and we could help them advertise their businesses if they could support us with a little share of their wares to help our production. Our home economics teacher, Mrs. Nanbam, was one of our regular targets for these adverts, and she often responded positively. She made buns, Nigerian egg rolls, and drinks. This minor change rejigged the press club advertising arm and opened the door for people to try new things.

The most impactful thing we did was to bring back Press Club Week. A week-long event, Press Club Week was dedicated to highlighting the activities of the club. The event would conclude with a festival of eating, dancing, and celebration. Since the founding of the press club six years before my time, only one Press Club Week had been held. There were many good reasons why the event had ceased, but when we came on board, we decided we would hold one no matter what. The Vice President played a significant role in making this a reality. While I had the ideas of what to do and why to do it, she had the practical common sense of how to do it. It was all thanks to her that it happened. She knew how to raise funds, how to convince the school to grant us a day, and how to motivate the students to cooperate successfully.

The previous administrations could not hold a Press Club Week because it clashed with the school calendar and cost the school a lot of money. But Faith, my VP, was able to remove much of the expense from the school's responsibility and bring it back to the press club itself. She implemented an effective membership dues program and sourced funds from older students and teachers. With this, she solved a challenging problem. As for a day that fit into the calendar, the planning began several months ahead. We fixed the date and walked backward to it. The strategy was a success.

I read a book that impressed me a few months before Press Club Week. It was a book by Amma Darko titled *Faceless*. The book follows the story of children on the streets of a slum named Sodom and Gomorrah who had no protection from family or society, and told of the tragic death of Baby T. I could relate to the book because Jenta was also a slum. People have even used the names Sodom and Gomorrah to describe Jenta. Faceless showed me the probable fate of kids in Jenta if things didn't change. I couldn't do much, but I could begin to create awareness. The theme for the Press Club Week event of that year became "The Future of The Nigerian Child." Amma Darko's *Faceless* inspired it. It was not the last time that a book would motivate me to take action.

The guest speaker for the final day of Press Club Week was a certain Mr. Samuel Wallangko. He came and delivered a powerful speech that moved us to a standing ovation. My only regret is that the event targeted the children, not the adults responsible for creating a better world for them. With the program's success, there was increased interest in Press Club amongst the students. Many more wanted to join, and we welcomed them.

There was still the nagging problem of how to source the news. I came up with a classic Lengdungian solution. It solved the problem my way but violated the established authority's rules and created even more problems. After Press Club Week, we raised a substantial sum by the previous standards of the club. It was enough money to buy us a phone. But getting a phone was one thing: I would have to get permission from the school to operate one for the club, and the phone would have to be with a staff member, preferably the patron of the press club. When we went home for a break, I returned with a phone with the plan that the press club would pay me for it and use it for the club. I did not get permission to do that or inform the press club patron about my plan. I brought the phone, which stayed with me for several weeks. I held the phone partly out of sheer desire to break the rules and partly because I was waiting for my Vice President to resume and give me money for the phone before I relinquished it to the Press Club. Without the money, I couldn't submit the phone to an authority. Hence, I was holding an illegal property. She resumed school many weeks after resumption date. Up until that time she had been my greatest help, now she would become my Achilles heel. We used the phone efficiently for the news gathering during the few weeks when it was with me. I was pleased with the results.

Sometimes, the law catches up with you faster than you would imagine. One night, we were in class having our evening preps when a group of teachers came into the class and started searching every student: their pockets, their lockers, their bags, everything. As soon as I saw them, I dropped the phone at the last seat in the class. One of our teachers found it and picked it up. He asked the class, "Whose phone is this?" Everyone was silent. We were a pretty cooperative bunch. He asked again, "Whose phone is this?" Everyone was silent. He shook his head in a way that indicated a threat and asked again, "For the last time, whose phone is this?" Of course, this man was Mr. Aminu, the same man who had inaugurated me into boarding school with a sound lashing.

As a last resort, he turned on the phone and dialed a number in the previous calls. He gently told the person that someone had found the phone on the road and they were searching for the owner. The guy on the other end said, "Oh, thank you so much. The phone belongs to my friend Lengdung. Please keep it for him." Mr. Aminu thanked the guy, whose name was John Smiles. That day, John removed the smile from my face. Our physics teacher, Mr. Mapis, who had been standing close to me, slapped me with his hand and booted me with his feet. He was outraged that I was even daring to play them. Despite this call, I denied that the phone was mine. They beat me badly, hoping I would concede. I didn't.

For many days, the school authorities did nothing about our case. Then, one day during classes, I was called to the office of the Disciplinary Committee. I knew what was up. I had thought about it for a long time already. When I entered the office, one staff member looked at me and said, "You know why you are here, don't you?"

I said, "Yes."

He asked, "Whose phone is this?"

He had expected some denials and some arguments.

Instead, I answered, "It is my phone, sir."

They were stunned. They didn't expect an easy interrogation. They asked if I had anything more to say. I didn't, and I told them so. I realized my explanation wouldn't make sense to this group of teachers. My judgment had been coming for a long time. They had not been comfortable with me as I was a constant contrarian. Rumors had gone around the school the previous week that the disciplinary committee had already decided I needed to be dealt with and put in my place. They had gotten a big fish and wanted to set an example. There was no escape for me. It took a few more days, and then there was a call for a sudden general assembly. We all knew something was wrong. The previous day, my favorite teacher, Mr. Chinnan, called me to deliver the bad news that the school would suspend me and withdraw my prefectship. He mentioned that the disciplinary committee had considered an expulsion but couldn't follow through as I was in my final year. I thanked him for the news and returned to the hostel. So, when the bell rang, I knew what it was about. We marched to the assembly ground and went through the usual routine of teachers exhorting students to keep quiet. Then, our Principal Admin took the stage and gave some preliminary words on discipline, obedience, and the responsibility of leaders. He announced that some students were found guilty and called their names, their crimes, and their punishment. When the Principal Admin got to the last name, he heaved a sigh of disappointment and called, "Lengdung Apolos." The students gasped in surprise. He announced that I was suspended for two weeks, stripped of my prefectship, and ordered to serve punishment after I returned from suspension. There was noise from the students, mostly of surprise and anger. No one had previously been punished so severely for bringing a phone to school. Secondly, some of them knew why I brought the phone to school.

I was to leave school the next day. That evening, I received more letters than ever during my entire school stay. Letters came from all corners, both boys and girls, juniors and seniors. Some expressed a feeling of unfairness; others reminded me that all things happened for good. I read them and cried. When I returned to the hostel that evening, I met Mr. Matthew Barde, my school guardian. That evening, he had no words for me. I knew he was disappointed. I was disappointed, too. Disappointed in my life. That night, the thought that dominated my mind was how I would face my dad. How could I tell him I was suspended? How could I tell him I was suspended for taking a phone to school when he had never bought one for me? These thoughts tore me up inside.

The next day, I packed my bag and headed home. I wasn't sure I would return. It was common for students not to return when suspended because they felt so much shame. On getting home, I gave my dad the letter that the school gave me for him. He had expected it would be another school fee payment reminder. When he found out it was a suspension letter, he heaved a sigh of relief. Then he began to probe. Surprisingly, I gave him answers without holding back. He was the first adult to whom I explained my thought process about the whole situation. More surprisingly, he understood and believed me. For the first time in our relationship, we spoke like grown men to each other. He made it clear that I was wrong even though the school was rather harsh in its judgment. Then, in the end, he said, "You fought for the right cause in the wrong way."

Wow! That was more than good news to my ears. My dad understood me.

After two weeks, I returned to school with my sister. When students saw me from the gate, there were voices all around hailing me and telling each other, "SP is back! SP is back!" SP means Senior Prefect. It was a touching reminder of the other side of my punishment: I was no longer the senior prefect. I went with my sister to the Principal's office, received some advice, and my sister made a commitment as my guardian that I would abide by the rules of the school authority. Soon, she left me to deal with my shame. The shame I felt was reasonable. Once you are suspended, you have been marked as a criminal. Now, I was a criminal. Nothing could be worse than such an indictment in a Christian school where outward morality meant so much. My friends were very supportive and reminded me that I was still their SP no matter what.

My relationship with many teachers changed dramatically, however. The title of Senior Prefect came with some privileges and respect. With it gone, most teachers removed the respect and privileges. Some even went beyond, using every opportunity to remind me of how far I'd fallen. They punished me severely at every opportunity. I was lucky that this happened during my last months in the school, as it would be over soon. So, I resolved that for the rest of my stay in school, I would pursue only one goal: to be the best graduating student in my class. I read like crazy. I no longer had the responsibilities that could bog me down, so I gave reading my everything.

When graduation day came, it began as usual with JSSS1 class. The best students in each subject were called, the student received their prize and returned to their seat, and if a student was a best student in more than one subject, they would return again. It went on this way up to SSS3.

"The best student in English Language, Lengdung Tungchamma." I walked up to the stage to receive my prize. But before I could walk back to my seat, the announcer spoke again.

"The best student in Mathematics, Lengdung Tungchamma."

"The best student in Further Mathematics, Lengdung Tungchamma."

"The best student in Civic Education, Lengdung Tungchamma."

"The best student in Data Processing, Lengdung Tungchamma."

"The best student in Biology, Lengdung Tungchamma."

"The overall best graduating student, Lengdung Tungchamma."

I won the most prizes in my class and received the Best Graduating Student Award.

Something important had also happened in the final months of school. The Principal Admin, Mr. I. D. Silas, who was responsible for decisions such as suspensions of students, invited me to his office. It was the first time we were conversing on a personal level. He asked about my life. Unlike me, I opened up to him about everything, and he eventually asked about the phone episode. I explained the details as truthfully as possible. He had been a Press Club member in his school days, and we used his house to write news sometimes. He understood me very well. At the end of the conversation, he told me I would be restored to my prefectship, if not for anything, for the sake of the symbolism. He said I was too gifted to waste my potential chasing useless goals. The school restored my prefectship the following week. Now, the name SP had a new meaning. To this day, I meet people who call me SP. I was the special one. The only SP to have been suspended. The only SP to have been removed and reinstated.

I will never forget what Mr. Silas did for me. He rescued me from a place of deep regret. His words encouraged me to chase my goal of being the best graduating student. Some teachers may never teach you in a class, but they will shape your life for decades. Some years after graduating, he became the first figure I was interested in writing a biography of. He had been the principal of a different school before coming to All Nations Academy. In that school, he had grown the membership from less than a hundred to more than a thousand. He had taken the school from no reputation to one of the most reputable schools in the entire state. Christ Apostolic College, Kuba, was a household name when he left. A few years after our graduation, we got the news that Mr. Silas had been in an accident and died while en route to the hospital. He had always loved traveling and had a special bag containing every basic necessity for living; he was always ready to be on the road. Mr. Silas had died doing what he loved to do. The impact of his life is present in the lives of hundreds of students like me, whom he shaped for the better.

My suspension from ANA was nothing unique for a Jenta kid. Yes, it was horrible and had devastating effects, but to be suspended or expelled was just part of the expected narrative. I could have accepted my fate as a typical rebellious kid and continued down my Lengdungian path; however, the actions of Mr. Silas gave me a new perspective. I saw that the school had forgiven and restored me; now

I owed the school—and I owed myself—the responsibility to make the most of my second chance. This was the mindset that guided me till my graduation. Again, unlike many other Jenta kids who didn't receive such second chances, I was lucky. I know of kids suspended from school, which ended their education. To their parents, the fact that they couldn't focus and study was proof that they weren't serious; it was better for the family to save the money used for school and use it on other things rather than waste it on a child who wasn't serious about education. Jenta is a harsh place with very few second chances.

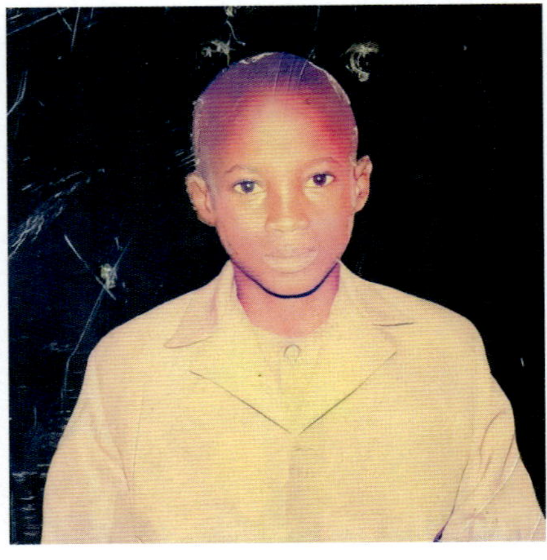

Above: Lengdung age seven

Right: Wearing the uniform of the
Police Children School, age twelve

Left: Lengdung's father and
three of his sisters at the time
of this writing

Below: Aunty Paula

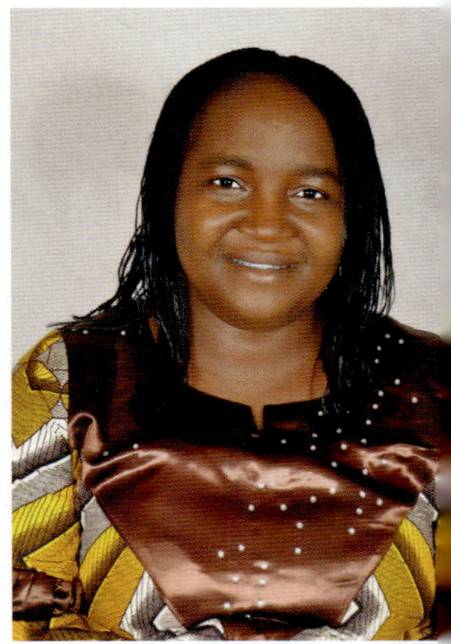

Lengdung's mother, to whom this book is dedicated

ll Nations Academy Antics
ndy Dayak (right), the infamous "Pot
riminal." Lengdung is behind.

ANA Graduation Portrait
Lengdung is eighteen years old.

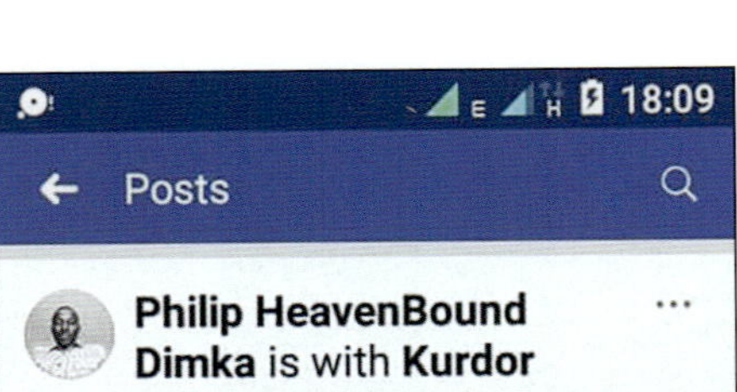

Above: Philip Dimka's confident Facebook post that resulted in the Jenta Reads Community Initiative

Above right: Water delivery, an early community service project of the Jenta Reads Community Initiative

Middle: Thaine Norris, on his first visit to Jenta, with Lengdung Tungchamma and Philip Dimka, sitting under the mango tree at Mama Goma's

Bottom: Lengdung and Philip, outside the small space donated by Mr. Justin, holding book boxes that Thaine brought as luggage on his first visit to Jenta

Above left: The prize that funded the new library facility, a place that has become a community hub, changing the narrative of Jenta

Above right: The Jenta Reads Community Library, nestled in the rocky hills of Jenta Mangoro

Middle: Eb Roell teaching Philip Dimka how to play chess

Bottom left: Chess champion Nathan Abok, who learned how to play at the Jenta Reads library

Bottom right: Bob and Meredith DeVoe participating with an addiction recovery group at the Jenta Reads library

Above: Here preparing for one of his first presentations about Jenta Reads, Lengdung now speaks frequently about the merits of reading and about grassroorts communtiy transformation. In conferences, schools, radio programs, a TEDx talk, podcasts, and now a memoir, he loves to inspire others to lift their gaze above their circumstances.

Left: The vibrant Jenta Reads community volunteers. Among the many pictured are: Manna Mamfat, Lekzy Gaknung, Peace Emmanuel, Zingit Goma, Daniella Minaan, Lilia James, Longdi Sylvanus, Agnes James, and Andrew Wumanna.

Above: Presenting the new library to Jenta community leaders. From right to left: Philip Dimka, Peter Kurdor, Stephen Longkat, Emakpo Joseph, Timothy Eneche, Israel Dimka, Shedrach Deshi, Lengdung Tungchamma, Rotji Joseph, Supreme Gilbert, Timchang Wazhi, Christopher Manga, Gana Musa

Right: Peter Kurdor, Erika and Thaine Norris, Eb and Debbie Roell, Lengdung and Senfat, with Jukgak Goma behind

Below left: Bob DeVoe praying for marriage blessings and more books

Below right: Feyishayomi Ayo with some of the books from the Jenta Reads Essential Library

CHAPTER 9

GLIMPSES OF ANOTHER WORLD

Throughout my stay at All Nations Academy, I tried to dictate the rules of engagement. I did not accept the school's ways or their wisdom; my ongoing war against the establishment. But once in a while, the establishment would win a battle.

Terrible tragedies around me, watching my Christian teachers fail, and constantly being bombarded with rote religion made me skeptical. I was especially skeptical of everything that suggested the supernatural. Despite my skepticism, one experience at All Nations Academy remains a formative point in my life.

Like my church at home in Jenta, All Nations Academy also had a branch of the New Life For All (*Sabon Rai* in Hausa) group. However, at ANA, the group was focused solely on singing every Sunday since the school was a closed campus, which didn't allow opportunities for outside evangelism. During the week, there was a prayer meeting, and once every month, the whole group fasted and prayed.

One of these monthly Sabon Rai fasting and prayer meetings was especially noteworthy. It was in my third year at All Nations Academy. During the prayers, after fasting from morning till late afternoon, the group began by reading Acts 1:5-8. Verse eight says, "But you will receive power when the Holy Spirit comes on you; and you will be my witnesses in Jerusalem, and in all Judea and Samaria, and to the ends of the earth."

The thinking that day was that the Sabon Rai group existed to evangelize those who didn't know Christ. But had the Spirit of the Lord come upon the Sabon Rai members? Had they received power? And most importantly, could they receive power? With these humble questions in mind, they prayed to God, acknowledging their weakness. While waiting for God's answer, the group decided they would not leave the meeting hall until the Spirit of God visited them. A prayer meeting that typically lasts for one hour became a program lasting from 3 pm to 6 am.

Between 10 pm and 6 am, something extraordinary happened.

It began without any drama. Group members were praying, crying, and pleading for God's mercy. The group confessed its unworthiness in carrying Christ's message, being His ambassadors, and representing Him in the world. If He would not empower them, they would be unable to do His work.

Then, around 10 pm, a voice broke out at the back of the hall with strange sounds. Before long, another voice broke out. It became evident that they were speaking in unknown languages, and then another group member stood up and began interpreting what they were saying. That was the turning point. The whole nature of the meeting changed. The gifts of the Spirit appeared one after the other: words of wisdom, words of knowledge, faith, and others.

This meeting was held within the class premises, a considerable distance from the dormitories. The regular students had returned to their rooms for the day, leaving the class premises empty between 10 pm and 6 am, except for the Sabon Rai. When students returned the next day for the morning devotion, they found the Sabon Rai members still praying.

It was a strange sight. News began to spread around the school that there were some "Holy Holy" who had prayed from 3 pm to 6 am. They had missed their lunch and dinner and were still praying.

The news traveled fast in a small place like All Nations. By afternoon, it was the hottest topic amongst the students. I had no opinion about the group at first. I told others they were fanatics who didn't know what to do with their time. That afternoon, the Sabon Rai met again, and again, they prayed from 3 pm to 6 am. The prayer meetings went on for four days. By then, nobody could ignore it. Something was clearly going on here. Even more intriguing was that all those who attended these sessions came out with visible joy on their faces. They may have been physically tired, but still, they were enthusiastic about the prayer session and God. And they would keep going back. Many curious students would visit the hall during the praying to see the spectacle. I noticed that some of these students would go in and not return till the next day. Even some of my friends had gone in and didn't return until the next day. I asked them what had happened, and they had no explanation. I would mock them and say they lacked the mental grit to withstand simple hypnotism. My church background in Jenta was not charismatic. My church taught that the signs and wonders celebrated in the Pentecostal churches were heretical. Besides, I was extremely uncomfortable with such things.

On the fifth day, I decided to see things for myself. At least I wanted to confirm the nonsense for what it was. Usually, one could peep through the window and see what was happening. But from the outside, we couldn't see anything extraordinary occurring. There were just students kneeling, lying down, some rolling on the floor, and others crying, singing, or praying. I went in, found a place at the back, and just sat watching. The simplicity of the meeting struck me. Nothing supernatural or magical was happening. From time to time, a person would walk to the center and share a bible passage, a prayer request, or make a confession. Then, he would return to his seat. Someone else might take his place, or everyone might remain seated for a while, praying, singing, and otherwise just enjoying the presence of God. The confessions affected me. Students were confessing things that I could never imagine them confessing. Reconciliations were happening right there in the hall. Student A would admit she was envious of student B and ask for forgiveness right there. Student B would accept the apology, and the two would hug with the warmest embrace I had ever seen. Students confessed to stealing, sneaking out of school, avoiding responsibilities, and many other things.

I do not remember at what point I broke down. It was the confessions that got to me. What about me, who had done far worse things than these students? As they walked to their seats with evident joy after their confessions, my own depravity became more and more apparent to me. My sin was crystal clear in contrast to theirs. I did not walk to the center to confess my sins, but at my seat, conviction brought me to tears. I asked God for mercy. While praying, I felt a hand on my shoulder. It was a senior named Israel Jeremiah. He spoke to me gently and said, "God has heard you. He loves you beyond any sin you've committed." I was not even on speaking terms with Israel before that day. We weren't friends. But God had spoken to him to give me a message.

I stayed through that night and returned the next day, and I kept returning every day till the end. As the days progressed, we explored the gifts of the Spirit and the fruits of the Spirit. Amongst Pentecostal Christians, at least in Nigeria, the external, showy gifts of the Spirit are emphasized, while the less obvious, internal fruits of the Spirit are not. But during these weeks, the fruits of the Spirit were as prominent as the gifts. Jesus said that we will be known by our fruits (not by our gifts). Living together as we did put these things to the test. We could not speak in tongues and then use the same tongue for foul or unkind language. We could not speak words of wisdom and then tell lies with the same tongue. There was a significant change in this regard. We became kinder, gentler, more peaceful, and more patient. We made sacrifices that would hurt us but protect other students. Living packed together in a boarding house like All Nations Academy was a situation where the worst in people came out. But during those weeks, the best of us was on display. Our lives were preaching the sermons.

The prayers continued for weeks on end. It became a part of the daily routine. But eventually, some teachers complained that it was interrupting the regular school schedule. They complained at staff meetings and to Principal Adisa. It was then that Adisa reminded the teachers of the history of the school.

We discovered that All Nations Academy was established after such an event. Before the school existed, young people gathered annually in Bokkos to pray. The Spirit of God would work amongst them powerfully. After a few years, they decided to make the place a permanent meeting location, so they purchased the property as All Nations Gospel Ministry. Not long after that, they started a school. All Nations Academy was the product of All Nations Gospel Ministry, an outgrowth of revival and young people searching for God. Twice a year, major events at the property included prayer meetings, sermons, and Bible studies. These events were well attended, with people traveling from all over the Bokkos Local Government. The December program was the largest. Sometimes, up to three thousand people could be present. These programs were power-packed, and when they finished, the people left with a palpable sense of God's presence. When they returned home, new revivals would often spark in the villages. Reports from these programs spread around Bokkos like wildfire; stories of redeemed families, restored relationships, changed lives, and even physical healings were numerous. In my final year at All Nations, a new student came to write our final exams. Henry Nwafor was rewriting after a ten-year absence from school. We became close, and I learned his story. He had been a member of a gang for many years and had committed many brazen robberies. His activities were so reckless that his fellow gang members decided to get rid of him. He ran away to his village in Bokkos. While there, he heard about the popular annual conference at All Nations Academy, so he decided to attend. The sermons, the worship, and the whole experience set him on a path to a different life. Now, he wanted to be a changed man, so he began by going to all his former victims, apologizing, and making restitution. Eventually, he realized that to move forward in life, he would need to return to school. Why not All Nations Academy, the same place where he had encountered Christ?

His story was not unusual. Thousands came to the conference every year and many had the same experience. It was the thing that built the reputation of All Nations Academy and that compelled my mother to send me there. All Nations Academy was well known as the place where academic, intellectual, and spiritual transformations occurred, with the spiritual transformation being the most celebrated aspect of the school.

During my years at All Nations Academy, I made sure to dodge these annual conferences, even though they were compulsory for certain classes. It was one of the rebellious actions I took against the system. But apparently, even I didn't escape the fruits of it, which followed me right into the school term.

Did the experience change me? Not really. For the period that the revival was active, about three months, my life was different, and my classmates commented on it. I was more tolerant, more understanding, less troublesome, and often a peacemaker. The voice of God was constantly in the background, guiding me and reminding me of the new life I should live up to. However, we went home for vacation, and when I returned, the spiritual fire had gone out, and I returned to my old Lengdungian ways. At this time, a lady from my tribe told my classmates that my name, when split into two syllables, meant "spoiled soup." When they wanted to hurt me, they would say, "He is a spoiled soup. Can you repair a spoiled soup? There's no hope for him."

I had doubted the wisdom of All Nations Academy; I had bucked the system for years. But in the end, the benefit of hindsight has allowed me to see the personal transformation that started there. The school sowed the seeds of that transformation. All Nations Academy gave me a solid concept of a good life, a solid foundation in the knowledge of God, and a solid worldview that would become more important in the years to come. I owe a debt I cannot pay, although I did not know I owed that debt for several years.

After reading the story of my spiritual encounter, you might have thought God would have fixed my life permanently. Most people would have preferred a story that went from "Bad Guy" to "Born Again" to "New Life Forever." But that is not my story. I wish I could have lived a righteous life consistently from that point on, but I guess I was too human, too imperfect, a bit of spoiled soup.

CHAPTER 10

The Church, Churched, & Unchurched

The church was the heart of the community and our lives. At the church, a child is presented to the community for the first time, he is baptized there when he turns eighteen, and later it hosts his wedding. All of us have beautiful memories of the church.

You spent part of nearly every day at the church, attending multiple weekly meetings. There, you learned about God, the creation of the world, the fall of man, the calling out of Abraham, the creation of the nation of Israel, its journey through the wilderness, and its survival. Although we did learn some stories from the New Testament, mainly during Christmas and Easter, the church drew most of its teachings from the Old Testament. The church taught us about the Almighty God, portraying Him as a dominating figure focused on legalistic righteousness and eager to punish wrongdoers. Perhaps this flowed from our culture, a culture of honor and shame. My conception of God during these years was just the kind you would meet in the Old Testament after a simple reading: He was after my life, not friendly, and constantly watching to see where I was wrong so he could punish me.

I assure you, the Bible contains some of the greatest stories ever told. Whether you read it as a single book or as individual books, you come away feeling the fire. If you want stories of stubborn children and disobedient teenagers, you will find them there. If you are looking for tales of kings and their battles, you will find them there. There are stories of love, adventure, hope, and everything in between. Having a good storyteller as your teacher in Sunday school is truly a blessing. Such a teacher makes the stories come alive. Some teachers were not merely good storytellers; they were dramatists. They acted out the Bible passage as they narrated it. It was a delight. These tellings enriched my imagination and enlarged my world.

We had great respect for the church. It was a sacred place where you wouldn't do the things you do elsewhere. It was out of our respect for the church that we bathed before we went there. We dressed in our best clothes, ensured we looked decent, and then headed to the temple of God.

It was also in the church that I found the opportunity to show off some interesting habits I had picked up as a teenager. One of these was the Nigerian practice of arriving late for events. Arriving late is commonly seen as a sign of prestige. Dignitaries would arrive late to an occasion, and the MC would explain their lateness and offer an apology so that the attendants understand that the big man was very busy, and couldn't make it on time. The attendants would feel lucky that he had chosen to make himself available to them for that occasion despite his busy schedule.

This attitude has permeated almost all Nigerian cultural life. Very few people want to be the first at events or programs. As a teenager, I picked up the clue that arriving late for events was a sign of status. Although I was not high class, I figured people would think of me as high class if I could be late. Every Monday, we attended Bible Study Fellowship. At the end of each quarter, we had a grand finale, which included a buffet service where you could eat your fill. I dressed in my finest clothes for this grand finale and headed to the venue. Although

I arrived late, they seated me in the front because all the back seats were already taken. When it was time for the meal, the main event of the day, I decided to flaunt my fake status. I informed the usher I would go last so others behind me could flow. They went ahead and served themselves. Sitting in my seat, I could see how attendees filled their plates. A girl would come and get a slice of pizza, shawarma, some spoonfuls of rice, spoons of beans, spaghetti, and a bottle of soft drink. As I watched this, I realized I was in deep soup. I was going to have nothing at the end of the day. But now, I couldn't tell the usher I wanted to go immediately. I still wanted to maintain my artificial status. I kept my game, and eventually, my turn came. But all that was left was water. That day, I learned the crucial lesson that fake life (a deceitful lifestyle) doesn't bring you anything, not even food. It also showed that human nature was the same everywhere; one can find the attitude of excess consumption in the church and any other kind of gathering. Humans are the same, after all.

In Sunday School, I learned a big secret that notorious children do not share with anyone else. We were taught from a young age to always give to God. They taught us that God doesn't need our offering, but we give it to Him anyway to show that our hearts are committed to His work. We also learned to give in support of our pastors. Pastors are kind; their work is just to teach us, so who will pay for them to feed their families? It made sense. Give to God every Sunday. Your offering belongs to God, and you are not supposed to touch it. But one day, another rebellious kid in Sunday School impressed something upon me: GOD DOESN'T NEED OUR OFFERINGS! I've always heard it, but it came hard and clear this time. GOD DOESN'T NEED OUR OFFERINGS! Well then, since God doesn't need our offerings, I need them. I have plans. There are sweet digestive biscuits that I want to consume. But still, the pastor needs offerings. So, I reached a compromise. I would give half of the offering, and then I would keep half. Done deal. Everyone was happy.

But there was one problem. The offering always came from my parents to me and then to God. In a real sense, it wasn't my money. One Sunday, I was returning home from Sunday school, and as usual, I had bought my favorite biscuit. Coincidentally, as I was enjoying it, I encountered my mother on the way home.

"Who gave you that biscuit?" she asked.

"No one," I replied.

"Then how did you get it?"

Silence.

You see, my mum was a part-time investigator. She never left anything halfway done. She began to dig and trace. Eventually, the other boy with whom we bought the biscuits exposed us. That day God forgave us, but Mother punished us. To be fair to her, it was her money.

Duped in Church

A big event for the church boys is the annual Boys' Brigade Week. It begins on a Monday and ends on a Sunday with a glittering parade. Activities for the week include the parade, football games, bible lessons, bush camps, and fundraising. Fundraising was the most demanding of all the activities. We used the Boys' Brigade week to raise funds for the needs of the Boys' Brigade group. For years, one significant need had been a drum set. Often, we relied on borrowed drums for our parades. We set the target of buying drums year after year, but this was challenging due to Jenta's poverty.

After saving for three years, we were close to our goal.

The year 2013 was going to be the year. We were sure we would get it that year if we did everything right. We had a format for the fundraising. We would go house to house in the community, targeting the wealthier community members. We would begin by cleaning their compounds, sweeping, washing plates, moving heavy equipment, running errands, and sometimes even washing clothes. After finishing, we pulled out our information sheet and presented our case to the house residents, explaining our needs.

This strategy served us well. In my group, we visited seventy houses, and almost all of them were in the wealthy category. The donations we received included some 1,000 naira notes and 500 naira notes. These were the highest denominations in Nigeria. Amongst the different groups within the Boys' Brigade, our group had done far better than all the others. Other groups received donations in 200 naira notes, 100 naira notes, 50 naira notes, and even 5 naira notes. We returned to the church late and were instructed to head home and come back tomorrow with our report and cash in hand. It was an ecstatic feeling. We had done it. We had raised enough money to cover the cost of our drums. The Boys' Brigade in other churches used to mock ours because we had no drums, but this would end. A new chapter would begin for us.

We returned the next day, and our group had a final meeting before submitting our report when we noticed something unusual. Somebody had changed the money recorded on the sheets. 1,000 naira had been changed to 100 naira. One zero had been canceled out. 500 naira was changed to 50, and so on. When we counted the cash at hand, it had also changed in tandem with the changes made on the record sheet. We were outraged. What iniquity was this? How can someone be stealing from the work of God? I was so pissed off that I reported it to our captain. Our captain looked at our records briefly and decided to ask our group leader what happened. The leader said the money given to him was the money he reported. He swore that he didn't change anything. I tried hard to convince our captain that the changes were noticeable.

In the argument that ensued, my group members gradually grew silent. At first, they confirmed everything I said and were also angry. But then the captain changed his tone and began using his authoritative voice. They gradually grew silent and started deferring to our group leader. I was so outraged. I said many things about how the leaders couldn't even live up to the creed they were teaching us. I felt disappointed that someone taught the values of the Boys' Brigade would steal, and even more so that the captain believed the deception simply because the group leader was a senior.

I was enraged at the group leader and the captain and soon became angry at the church. If I couldn't see honest people in the church of God, then why the heck was it called a church in the first place? How could a church leader be this hypocritical? I thought the church was supposed to be where I found people I could admire. This episode added more to my growing case against God and His people. How could He allow such fake people to carry His name? How could He watch as poor boys were being duped?

I left the Boys' Brigade that day and never returned. I also began to distance myself from the church. Although I still attended church, as was expected in a "Christian community," I was no longer enthusiastic about it. It had become meaningless. I told myself that those fake people could not teach me how to live.

Saint Lengdung

By the time I was in JSS3, I had given my life to Christ many times. When we entered JSS1, one of the buzz phrases we encountered was "giving your life to Christ." I came from a highly orthodox church, and they hardly used these phrases. However, at All Nations Academy, almost every Sunday, there was a guest speaker who called for students to give their lives to Christ. The preacher would elaborate that giving your life to Christ was something you needed to do to be safe. Sometimes, the preacher would urge us to renew that commitment. The sermon went something like this:

"You've sinned, and you need to be saved and cleansed. This is your last chance."

The sermon would end with the preacher asking,

"What would happen if you died right now, and where would you go?"

I didn't want to go to hell. None of us wanted to go to hell. We would walk to the podium, confess our sins, and get a fresh start to avoid hell. As regular sinners, we had to do this often. The sweet icing of this whole process was the assurance of the preachers that God never gets tired of us and that He never gets frustrated with our constant failing and repentance. This message sunk in deep for me. I knew I could always walk to God and receive His forgiveness. Perhaps the message sunk deep because I was such a regular sinner. Weekend revivals were the blockbuster events of repentance.

The weekend revival was a once-in-a-term program. The school would invite a guest speaker from outside. Many times, these guest speakers would come with slide presentations. There was a particular preacher, Mr. Emmanuel Adeshina, who was the best of them all. He would begin his preaching by establishing the world's chaos, the four horsemen theory, explaining the imminent apocalypse, and ending with a call to commit to Christ. When Mr. Emmanuel finished, you felt sure that Christ would come tomorrow. How dare you not surrender your life to Christ? That weekend, there would be a lot of repenters. There would be new commitments, and some boy/girl relationships would break apart. Two weeks later, we would be right back where we were before the weekend revival. It was not because our commitments were insincere; it was because it was difficult not to be human.

Mother's Greatest Evangelism

Mother's most beloved mission field was her home. When my parents got married, my father was still an idol worshiper. He had not accepted the Christian faith. They had not married in the sense of a ceremony. They had eloped and left for the city.

Mother became interested in Christianity when they got to the city. Over time, she became committed and was baptized into the Christian faith. Father watched her in amusement. He wasn't interested. As far as he was concerned, he was from a royal family and ought to maintain and protect the traditions of his ancestors. These traditions were weird and sometimes dangerous. You could pull some of them straight out of the Old Testament. For instance, he would not hold any of his newborn children until three days after birth. But if he were not able to hold the newborn within seven days of birth, he could not hold the baby for the next three months. If a woman was on her period, she was not allowed to cook for him. He ate food only in a traditional deep dish known as a *kwarya,* a calabash.

As part of the royal family, he led the whole clan in the ritual sacrifices during festivals.

He was prone to anger and would react violently to problems. Once, he broke a television while he and his friends were watching a football match, and his team lost the game.

Mother lived with him this way. She believed he would change. She would often point to the story of St. Paul as an example, and waited for God to reveal Himself. Gradually, my father began to let go of his previous life. First, it was his anger that started to change. Instead of responding violently, he returned home and discussed the situation with Mother. She would listen, not judge him, and help him relax. Time did its work, and by the time he had finished explaining to her, his anger would have diminished significantly. Over time, they developed a strong rapport around this, making them best friends, and slowly his lifestyle changed. He threw away his kwarya. He ate Mother's food no matter when she cooked it for him. He reduced visits to the village, the place that made him partake in the traditional activities and festivals. Previously, when people went to church, he would go to the bush to collect herbal medicines. Now, he started attending church to listen to the sermons. He would return home and argue with Mother about the pastor's teachings. In 2010, he announced, to Mother's great joy, that he was joining the baptism class. She could not believe it. She told all of us and anyone else who cared to hear her. He was going to sign up in 2011.

Her evangelism of almost a quarter of a century would finally bear fruit. She mentioned that of all her mission work and church involvement, nothing would please her more than seeing her husband baptized in the church. Finally, it was going to happen.

Father was baptized in 2012. But Mother wasn't there. She died in 2011. He cried on that day. Her absence was sharper than anything.

Mother Traveled

It was a Saturday morning in 2011, and I was in the middle of a football game on the pitch at All Nations Academy. Suddenly, someone interrupted me with urgent news: Mr. Matthew, my school guardian, was calling me. He told me to get dressed and that he would take me home. At that moment, I didn't suspect anything. It was in the car that my thoughts began to run wild. All the "why" answers began to intrude.

When I left home for boarding school that term, Mother was pregnant. I began to wonder if she had given birth and they wanted me to be there for some ceremony. But the school authority was too strict to allow me to go home for something as trivial as that. So, if Mr. Mathew needed to bring me home, something more important had happened. But what? I just couldn't think of it. Moreover, my mind refused to accept the possibility of death. I dreaded the possibility of anyone close to me dying. Throughout the whole journey, Mr. Mathew was strangely quiet. This was the man I had known to be very inquisitive about me; he asked me questions whenever we met. But this time around, he was not asking anything at all. I had to live through the entire one-hour drive with increasing confusion and apprehension.

As soon as we got to Jenta, some women began pointing at me and saying, "Eyah, that is Lengdung. The only son of the house." What was going on? I desperately wanted to ask Mr. Mathew. Then he started talking.

"Are you a Christian?"

"Yes Sir"

"Are you sure?"

"Yes Sir"

"Have you made a commitment to Christ, given your life to Christ?"

"Yes Sir"

"Good. You understand that God is in charge of everything that concerns a believer. Is that correct?"

"Yes Sir, I do"

"God has a plan for everyone of us. Everything that happens to us is part of that plan. We may not understand it, we may not agree with it, but His plans are always beautiful in the end. He never leaves us or forsakes us. God says in the Bible..."

He did not finish his pitch before we reached the compound of our house, where a crowd was gathered outside. Crying.

Mother had died.

At that moment, I died, too.

Mother had died? No way.

Mother cannot die. Mother cannot die now.

Mother traveled.

Even as I write this, I am in tears. It is difficult to imagine that such a strong woman could die. She was always in control. She knew how to fix everything. She knew how to manage everything. I thought there was nothing beyond her. I was wrong. I learned that Mother had gone to deliver her eleventh child, but both Mother and her child did not survive. She had lost so much blood and needed a transfusion, but the doctors delayed because my father was not there yet.

Stupid.

During those first few days, I didn't want to do anything. I didn't want to talk to anyone, eat anything, or go anywhere. I didn't want to live. I asked God several times to take me, too. If Mother was not here, how then could I live? She was everything to me! My whole world! Literally. I was bitter and angry and ready to quit living. Consolers kept coming around to say, "Everything will be alright." "God will take care of you." "I understand what you feel. I've been there." I didn't believe any of them.

Nothing would be all right; nothing would ever be the same again.

I thought, *"You don't understand me. My mother is not your mother! God will not take care of me. If He would, why didn't He take care of Mother? If He could fail in caring for her, why should I think He will care for me? You are joking."*

I wanted to shout out these responses to the people who came around, but even more, I didn't want to talk. I just held them in my head. I was alone for several days. Although surrounded by neighbors and family members, I had never been more alone and disconnected. I stayed at home for one more week before returning to school. We traveled to Kanke to bury her. We, her direct children, sang a song in our dialect during the Sunday service, which, when translated into English, would mean,

"Mother, you are in heaven; we will see you someday."

I truly believed those words.

Something happened during the week that I was at home. One day, I dodged the crowd of people that had come to Mama Goma's house next door. Mama Goma was Mother's best friend for many years. I called her "Mother," too. Alone, lying on the bed, just wondering again, I noticed a big Bible on the far side of the bed. Out of boredom, I opened the last pages to read the concordance. I went straight to death. I found this passage which says;

"Listen, I tell you a mystery: We will not all sleep, but we will all be changed—in a flash, in the twinkling of an eye, at the last

trumpet. For the trumpet will sound, the dead will be raised imper-ishable, and we will be changed. For the perishable must clothe itself with the imperishable and the mortal with immortality. When the perishable has been clothed with the imperishable, and the mortal with immortality, then the saying that is written will come true:

'Death has been swallowed up in victory.'

'Where, O death, is your victory?

'Where, O death, is your sting?'

The sting of death is sin, and the power of sin is the law. But thanks be to God! He gives us the victory through our Lord Jesus Christ."

This was Paul's writing in 1 Corinthians 15:51-57.

These words began to change the way I was thinking about everything. I read other passages and began to understand the Christian view of death. It was a contrarian view. It turned everything on its head. What seemed apparent was that Mother was not completely gone. There was another chapter that would open up someday. Her exit from life was not the concluding words, "The End"; the story continues on another page. According to the Bible, this next page will be entitled "Heaven." Whatever that was, I wanted to be there. My new life mission was to live a life that would ensure I met with Mother someday. I wanted to be worthy to be joined together with her and Jesus.

Indeed, Mother had only traveled. I consoled myself with this.

A New Chapter in The Family

Before I could get to Mother in Heaven, I had to face a new chapter in the family. Our family dynamics had changed completely. Mother was everything. She had been the one person that held everything together. My father once told me that Mother was Mother even to him. He depended on her for so much. Father didn't believe he could live without her. At her funeral, he cried more than any of us. It was the first time I saw him crying. Father is a Stoic, a man of strong traditions. He believed men should not cry, and if he cried that day, it meant this touched him in a way that all his strength could not hold back.

Critically, the primary source of income for the family was the business Mother had established. In her absence, it began to crumble. Father was not good with handling a provision store, and the kids were more interested in looting the shop items. Inevitably, it started to decline. Eventually it closed permanently. It was unsustainable and had become a liability. When the business closed, our lives became more difficult.

Never in my life had I imagined that there would be a day when I would be hungry and not have something to eat. That day came, and many more. Father was trying his best. He maintained us in school and started doing many things I didn't normally associate him with, such as cooking for us. I had never imagined my dad as a chef, knowing that he was a very traditional man regarding gender roles.

Another area in which Mother's absence was evident was in the payment of school fees. Previously, I used to envy other kids sent home for failure to pay school fees. I would look at them and wish that I could also miss school. To me, this was an opportunity to play.

When Mother died, my school fees were delayed for the first time. The next term, the fees were not paid at all, and the school sent me home. I then realized that being sent home as a result of unpaid school fees was embarrassing rather than joyful.

As the names of the students who owed fees were called, you could feel the anger in the teacher's voice and the shame of all the other students staring at you. They would say, "This boy's parents are not even well-to-do. They can't even afford his school. Why did they put him in a school like this?" The way the teachers drove us out of class and the way other students looked at us gave us the feeling that we did not belong there. We were thieves, stealing education from a place that was not ours. I felt like an impostor, hanging out with other kids that were above me. Their parents were above my parents, their parents were doing better than my parents, their parents had things my parents didn't; and here I was, a poor Jenta kid, pretending to be in the same class with their kids.

When I got home, I was too ashamed to tell anyone else I was sent home for school fees. There was a sort of street code when anyone asked why you were not in school, and you said, "Nothing." They didn't press harder. They just assumed the lack of money kept you back home instead of being in school. I was not used to living by the code, but as the years passed and the absence of Mother became pronounced, I learned to live by it. I got accustomed to the code and taught it to other kids.

You can't do anything when sent home for school fees. You don't work. You don't earn any money. You are too ashamed to tell anyone. You have to wait for your parents. You learn to be helpless.

From my 3rd year to my 6th in Secondary, failure to pay fees was a regular part of my life at school. Eventually, I and a few others became so experienced at dodging the disciplinarians who would chase for the fees that we were teaching other students how to escape. In my final year, my father had to take a loan to cover my last school fees, it would take him almost a decade to pay it off. It was the only loan he had ever taken in his life.

Fresh Commitment

My final years in ANA were marked by lack of school supplies and many personal necessities. For three years I used the same uniform wearing it from Monday to Friday, and patching it up with thread and needle.

In my final year in ANA, something important happened on a particular Sunday. It was the third motion of my life, a decision that established a different path for my life. The first motion in my life was being sent away from Jenta for my secondary school, a movement that took me away from bad influences. Second, my suspension from school caused me to slow down, think about my life, and be more reflective, arresting the momentum toward selfishness. While these two motions happened to me, the third and most consequential motion was my decision.

On that Sunday morning we moved to the hall for Sunday service. The service went as usual: prayers followed by song demonstrations by the choir and other subgroups. The preacher preached and concluded by singing the hymn "Pass Me Not."

Pass me not, O gentle Savior
Hear my humble cry
While on others, Thou art calling
Do not pass me by

Savior, Savior
Hear my humble cry
While on others, Thou art calling
Do not pass me by

Let me at Thy throne of mercy
Find a sweet relief
Kneeling there in deep contrition
Help my unbelief

Savior, Savior
Hear my humble cry
While on others, Thou art calling
Do not pass me by

Trusting only in Thy merit
Would I seek Thy face
Heal my wounded, broken spirit
Save me by Thy grace

Savior, Savior
Hear my humble cry
While on others, Thou art calling
Do not pass me by

Thou the spring of all my comfort
More than life to me
Whom have I on earth beside Thee?
Whom in Heav'n but Thee?

Savior, Savior
Hear my humble cry
While on others, Thou art calling
Do not pass me by

My time at All Nations began to flash before my eyes. I had spent six years there. Sunday to Sunday, I heard the call to "Surrender your life to Christ," "Give your life to Christ," "Become born again," and all the other variations. In my early years, the words carried weight. I made commitments, but all of those were out of exuberance. As I understood the world and myself more, I moved away from these commitments and these beliefs. Christianity had become merely a religion to me. It was something I wrote on forms. It didn't have any bearing on my life. But now I began to think.

Was this how I wanted to go on into the wider world? Was this how I intended to return home? By the way, what had the life of rebellion brought to me? Disappointment from my teachers, the pain of regular punishment, constant restlessness, and a life I wouldn't be proud of if played for everyone on a large screen. And yet, what would Jesus do for me? Would he solve my problems? Would he fix the troubles I would meet at home when I returned? Well, Jesus had failed me once already. He allowed my mother to die even after she served him faithfully. She was committed to him in everything. She gave her all to him. Yet, when she needed him the most, he wasn't there. He couldn't, or wouldn't, keep her alive. Her death had brought so much suffering upon us. Jesus, why didn't you do something then? Why should I trust you to do anything now if you didn't do something then?

The words in the hymnals were speaking to me and leading me on.

"Help my unbelief."

"Heal my wounded, broken spirit

Save me by Thy grace."

And most importantly,

"Whom have I on earth beside Thee?"

Who would help me out of my misery? What options did I have? All the uncles who had come and promised to be of help to me after my mother's death were not present. So many people had promised things that never came to fruition. I knew then that I was alone. So, what would I do with my insignificant life?

That day, God did not pass me by. I knelt down and made a fresh commitment to Jesus. This time, it was going to be different. It was going to be a commitment with all my heart. Jesus would not be the historical figure; He would be my friend and Savior. I would live as He wanted me to live—or at least, I would try.

The Race to Heaven

Christmas was always colorful. It was the one day we all got to wear new clothes. No matter how poor your parents were, new Christmas clothes were necessary. You couldn't afford the shame of not having new clothes on Christmas day. No parents could withstand the ridicule that would be meted out on their family. So, some parents purposed to save Christmas clothes from January of the previous year. Other parents purchased Christmas clothes in July. Unsurprisingly, parents would have to buy oversized garments for their children with such a plan. How can clothes properly fit a child for twelve months of the year? The insurance was to buy bigger clothes.

Apart from once-in-a-while activities like the Christmas celebration, the church had a weekly timetable of regular activities. Women's Fellowship had their day of practice, and so did Men's Fellowship, choir, Boys' Brigade, Girls' Brigade, New Life for All, and all other church subgroups. In church, you moved in progressions. You began with Sunday School, then Boys' Brigade, then Youth Fellowship, and then probably choir or one of many other groups. These were effective tools for the socialization and development of the individual.

The Youth Fellowship, a group for ages fifteen to thirty, had the most significant impact on my life. We met every Monday and Wednesday from 6 pm to 7 pm. That one hour was often more enriching than all the previous hours of the day. In that one hour, I learned about life: God, society, government, wealth, relationships, and many other topics. The programs were designed to appeal to youth and to focus on youth issues. It was the only place I felt at home within the church during my teenage years. It was also the place that enabled my reconnection with Jenta after secondary school. There, I found good friends that would shape my future for good.

The decision to surrender my life to Christ at the end of my secondary school set the preamble for my participation in Church and Youth Fellowship in particular after graduating. If I had not given my life to Christ, there was little chance I would have taken the Youth Fellowship seriously. And without the Youth Fellowship, I probably would have encountered other circles within Jenta that would set me on the path to be a spoiled soup. Or maybe I would have come up with a Lengdungian solution again. There was a regular period of twelve months between graduating from secondary school and a tertiary education, I needed to fill that period with some activity. By making a commitment to Christ in that final year, I was making a commitment that had eternal consequences, but also had implications that bode well for me immediately, by keeping me from bad influences. At least in the Church, I would not be reintroduced to my former friends who smoke, abused drugs, and engaged in gang activities.

CHAPTER 11

NEW TURNS NEW LEAVES

During my secondary school years, my connections with many friends in the community became estranged. Leaving for school for most of the year and returning for brief holiday periods caused a chasm that could hardly be fixed for most of us. Some of them had also moved on to form other friendships. One of the few friendships that survived was with Peter Emmanuel. Peter attended day school while I attended boarding school. He was older than me by some years and was more of an elder brother. Even so, Peter was more mature than his age. His house was just a stone's throw from my house. He had a room to himself in his family's home. He was involved in several things that made his life more useful than many I saw in the community. He was a living embodiment of seeking knowledge by all means.

Another impressive characteristic Peter portrayed was his love for the practical application of knowledge. He had a balanced understanding of how the world worked. One time, I returned for holidays and saw that Peter had gotten a sewing machine. It turned out that Peter had been watching YouTube videos on sewing, and he became an expert at it just by watching. I would go to Peter's house because I had nowhere to go during those holidays. Peter's family always had more than enough food. If you dropped by, you were sure to get something to eat. Beyond physical food, Peter had another kind of food—books. I was hungry for distractions and for knowledge. Peter had a few books and could borrow almost any book from his friends.

One day, I visited, and he started talking about John Knox. I listened keenly for I was hearing new information for the first time. Next, he asked,

"Have you read about Martin Luther?"

"No," I replied.

"How about John Calvin?"

"No."

"Kathryn Kuhlman?"

"No."

"Take this," he said, handing me *God's Generals: The Roaring Reformers* by Roberts Liardon. I began reading the book right there in his room. After some weeks, I finished it and returned it. He gave me the next book. By that time, I was already deeply interested in the series. Unfortunately, he had just two of the books in the series. He made a promise to borrow the others on my behalf. He didn't get them during that holiday, but they were there when I returned four months later. I read them all.

Each time we conversed after I returned a book, I realized he had questions and thoughts as he read it. At that point, he attended a church open to conversations about the gifts of the Spirit. While my church was doctrinally conservative, he was not bulldozing me with his church experience; he was probing mine. He would ask "WHY" behind every act my church did. I hardly knew why.

We moved on from *God's Generals* to other books. He was always the one who got the books first, and he had all kinds of books. You could find Robert Greene's *48 Laws of Power* and *The Power of Positive Thinking* by Norman Vincent Peale. We would debate these ideas, argue them out, and sound each other out on conclusions we've arrived at. Robert Greene and Niccolò Machiavelli were two authors that I never cared to read from his shelf; I felt they didn't matter to me as I was no politician.

When I got a phone, Peter began sending audiobooks to my phone. Each time we met, and I asked for the latest music, he would instead use the opportunity to send an audiobook that he thought would be useful to me. I did not realize it then, but Peter was changing my world. He provided me with activities instead of joining others to roam the street and do nothing. One of the most important books we read then was *The Richest Man in Babylon* by George Samuel Clason. The book had a powerful effect on me, making me realize that I needed to do something to earn money and build wealth from there. My graduation from secondary school was not far off. What would I do to make money? What could I do? What opportunities could I try? These questions were on my mind as I returned to school.

Peter also began to invite me to programs that talked about purpose, destiny, vision, and all the other self-help topics. The first time he asked me, I gave him an excuse and told him I couldn't go. The next time, I came up with another excuse. One day, he asked what the real reason was. I told him I didn't have any clothes that would fit for this kind of event. It was true. Since Mother died, no one had bought new clothes for me. I had outgrown almost all the ones I had. Peter looked through his wardrobe and gave me some clothes. By the time I graduated from secondary school, more than half of my clothes were Peter's former clothes. I started attending a few of those programs. At first, I thought if I attended a program on purpose, the guest speaker would teach everyone exactly how to find their purpose. I thought it would be like;

Step 1: Go to a specific mountain.
Step 2: Check on the right side, and you will see your purpose.

In the case of building wealth, it would be like;

Step 1: Here is some money.
Step 2: Start a shoe business.
Step 3: Sell to people at Rayfield. Here are their contacts.
Step 4: Become a millionaire.

It was nothing even close to that.

What am I here for?

It was in Peter's room that I first saw *The Purpose-Driven Life* by Rick Warren. Rick Warren's book is a forty-day journey written to help you discover your life purpose. This book forced me to think critically about my purpose. What on earth was I here for? Why was I created? What does it mean to live a meaningful life? What is my relationship with God? The most important part about these questions was not the answers but the questions themselves. It was the first time I was putting myself in focus and asking provoking things. I had to confront myself, look back at my past self, and look at my future. Looking at my past, I had to confront the reality of my mother's death. For years, I had shelved it and ignored it.

After Mother's death, I learned to handle things by simply shutting down every emotion. In moments of pain or suffering, I believed I was alone. There was no point in telling anyone else. This process of shutting down soon extended even to emotions of joy. As I read Rick Warren, I had to go back to confront what had happened and what I had become since then.

In the first weeks after I returned to school after Mother's death, a teacher, Mr. John, had come to me to offer condolence.

"I'm so sorry for what happened. Take heart and be consoled that your mother is in a better place," he said.

"Thank you, sir."

"You are welcome. I hope you are doing fine?"

"To be honest sir, I am not fine. None of this makes sense. I cannot understand why my mum would be in a better place when we need her here more than anything. Did it have to be her?"

"Oh no," he interrupted me. "Don't say that. You can't question God. Everything that God does is for the best. He knows what's best for everyone. Do you know more than God? You don't. Just accept everything He does. Don't question Him."

He gave an almost complete sermon on why I shouldn't question God. He shared our conversation with other staff, and when they came to console me, they all said almost the same thing, harping on the message of not questioning God. I got the signal that questioning God or expressing dissatisfaction with Him was unacceptable.

I learned to keep my questions to myself. Rather than share my thoughts, I would mull over them and shut down. Soon, it became my coping mechanism. Absorb things, press them in, and never release them out. That's how I managed to live and survive whenever I faced a tragedy. And since the death of Mother, the tragedies only piled up. By the time I came to Rick Warren's *The Purpose-Driven Life,* I was a swelling balloon of pent-up emotions waiting for an explosion. Rick Warren's book ensured I didn't explode. Instead, I deflated gradually. The deflation began with his book, but it didn't end there. It continues today.

CHAPTER 12

Uncle Lewis, Anita, & The Café

Although I had given my life to Christ, my life was far from changed. My worldview, attitude, character, and everything else remained the same. The change had begun with Peter's friendship. The Youth Fellowship of my local church was another avenue God used to chisel out a different person from my past.

As we met every Monday and Wednesday, we talked about everything going on in our lives and the books we were reading. During our conversations, I became more familiar with the works of C. S. Lewis. I had an old laptop PC with a dead battery that still functioned as a desktop when there was power in Jenta. I downloaded C. S. Lewis's Chronicles of Narnia and began reading. It was so engaging that I read *The Horse and His Boy* within two days, and soon, I was plunging into the others.

One day, Philip Dimka came to the Youth Fellowship with a copy of *Mere Christianity* by C. S. Lewis. I was blown away. I picked it up several times just to admire it.

"Where did you get it?"

"Father's Bookshop."

"How much?"

"1500 naira."

1500 was all the money I could save if I didn't use my lunch money for a week. That's exactly what I did. I went without food, saved up for a week, and walked into Father's Bookshop to grab my copy. The date was 8th May 2017. I remember because I wrote it in the back of the book. It remains one of my treasures to this day.

Due to our shared passion for C. S. Lewis, Philip added me to a C. S. Lewis group on Facebook called "C. S. Lewis and His Master." In Jenta, models of the good life were scarce. We had many uncles and aunties, but few were heroes for the kind of ambition growing in us. Books fueled that ambition and provided the heroes. From works by C. S. Lewis to *God's Smuggler* by Brother Andrew, *Steve Jobs* by Walter Isaacson, and *Einstein* by Walter Isaacson, to several others, I discovered heroes I wanted to model my life upon. They inspired me and gave me a vision I could run with. Their characters, both good and bad, helped me set new standards for myself. The hard life of poverty all around me was still present, but now I was seeing new possibilities. Something different could happen. A man's birth did not determine his destiny. A man's past was not his fate. I also read another book, *Forgetting The Past,* by Bob Gass. It helped me tremendously in dealing with the past, both my misdeeds and the misdeeds I felt that life had thrown at me.

Around this time, I met an older lady who significantly changed my perspective and developed my character. Her name was Anita Clarkson. She was not old, but older than I was. Anita Clarkson was a lecturer at the Jos ECWA Theological Seminary (JETS). She also had a cyber café that had closed after the previous manager moved away. I did have some experience, so my friend Stephen recommended me to her as someone who had run a café previously. He also told her she would have a bookish companion. "Really?" she asked.

He went on to tell her how I read close to a hundred books every year. That was it. She hired me even before the job interview. The following week, I met with her to talk terms. We hardly spoke about the job; instead, we talked about books, books, and more books. I assumed my new job immediately. For me, it wasn't just a job but a mission. She mentioned that two other managers had tried to revive the place, but none had succeeded. I was determined to be the outlier. I wanted to succeed.

Well, I failed, and I failed miserably. Customers and revenue did not increase, and ultimately, I spent money trying to get things to work and didn't recoup it. We agreed that I would keep 50% of the profit every month. Since I had been spending money from my own pocket, it meant I lost money by the end of our partnership.

Despite the loss, I gained something more valuable—a friend. She was smart, she was open-minded, and she indulged me greatly. While working there, I looked forward to coming to work every day. Why? For the conversations, the camaraderie, and the books. As a lecturer, she had access to the famous Byang Kato Library in JETS. It was one of the largest theological libraries in Northern Nigeria. Through her, I could borrow books from the library. I got to see *Confessions* by St. Augustine for the first time in print. She also showed me works such as *The Imitation of Christ* by Thomas Kempis, *The Cloud of Unknowing*, and *Spurgeon Daily*.

Each day, when Anita returned from a class, she would get a seat in the café, eat lunch, and then try to prepare notes for the next day. She would often share her meals with me. One time, I asked her about the notes she was preparing. Thus began conversations on theological topics such as grace, sanctification, reformation history, predestination, and faith, amongst others. The subject that we spent the most time on was Grace. It was appropriate, as I needed Grace more than anything.

I had not understood why so many things had happened to me. I felt justified in some of the regrettable actions I had taken toward others. I felt that life's cruelty had made me a hard man. Being soft was a weakness, and I couldn't afford it. The best response to life and other human beings was more toughness, and I was ready to give it to them. Do to others before they do it to you. Why do some have an easy life while others do not? Why did God allow some people to die in earthquakes when they were His children? Why would God allow people to suffer when He could simply end it? Why would God allow people who had lived a good life to die early? Why would God allow my mother to die? Why? Why?

Anita didn't claim to have answers. Instead, she told me her story. She had gotten pregnant out of wedlock at the age of seventeen. Her husband, who was just a teenager, had promised to marry her. But her family did not approve of either the pregnancy or the marriage. She did not listen to them. Instead, she left and eloped with him. Within a few months, their marriage broke apart after he ran away from home, leaving her in his village. She was alone without any help and with in-laws who had not approved of their marriage in the first place. They mistreated her so much that she thought of killing herself. She didn't, and the baby in her womb kept her going.

Nine months later, she gave birth to a beautiful baby girl. Her in-laws rallied around her and received the baby with joy. Yet after a few months, they took the baby and chased her away. She could do nothing. She was in a village that was not her own, with no husband and sur-rounded by people hostile to her. They told her they would kill her if she ever set foot in their village again. She had no choice but to return home to her parents. Her family received her with much grumbling and zero sympathy. No one from her family joined her to fight for her baby. She lived with such agony for years, and eventually, she decided to run to the city. That was how she ended up in JETS.

When I met her, she was almost forty years old. She had no hus-band, could not reach her daughter, and was still trying to improve her life. Anita shared that upon arriving in the city, she found a church that supported her journey toward forgiveness for so many past wrongs and guided her toward healing. She blamed herself; the toughest part was forgiving herself. The experiences damaged her self-worth, and she used to be sensitive to what people said about her—but not anymore.

As we spent time together, her lifestyle did not seem like that of someone whose life had this magnitude of hurt. She had no bitterness, held no grudges, and was most likely to be the one to say, "Hey. Let's move on from this." She was firm but also gentle and kind. She was the kindest woman I had ever met. I asked her how her life had changed, and she responded, "God. He did it. He took a chance on me even when I wouldn't take a chance on myself."

In her library were many books by Philip Yancey: *Disappointment With God, What's So Amazing About Grace, Soul Survivor,* and *Where Is God When It Hurts.* She shared them with me and said we could talk after I read them. Within a few days, I finished *Disappointment With God.* I moved on to the next and then to the next until I read all of them. Now, I could see better. Yancey had written so well about Grace; he had helped me see a new perspective on Grace for myself and others. I saw a practical demonstration of it in the life of Anita Clarkson. She was the living embodiment of what Yancey had written.

"Now, I get it," I told her one day.

Pain is the window that God uses to reach the human heart. As C. S. Lewis described, pain is "God's megaphone for a deaf world." Suffering and pain were not God's plan for us, but every time we go through them, He has a way of turning each one around to hold a lesson or a blessing for us. We may not see it immediately when we are going through the episode, but we can trust Him. When we cry about the injustice in the world, we should remember that God's very own son came to this world and was unjustly killed on the cross. He was the most righteous of any man, yet He died. When we are angry at injustice, we should also remember that God was angry. When we are angry at pain, we should not forget that God's son went through pain.

So, who is going to fix this mess of humanity? Well, there are only two options. One is to believe that there will never be a fix, and the other is to believe in what Jesus did for us. Jesus promised that someday, all of this will be over. He promised that there is redemption. There is a whole new life. Someday, we will no longer have to endure suffering. The night will be over, and joy will come in the morning.

Working with Anita during those months unearthed the most concrete examples of Grace I had ever seen. She treated everyone with respect and was open to listening to others. Anita was not a person who would dismiss others when they complained to her. In Anita, I saw Grace in action.

One of the things I read in Philip Yancey's works was that whenever we cry out about the pain, suffering, and unending problems in the world, God responds. His response is us. Philip Yancey wrote a book entitled *Where is God When it Hurts?* and I have often asked the same question. The answer lies in another question, "Where is the church when it hurts?" We are God's response to a hurting world. He gave us—His children—as His answers to a world demanding answers. Anita Clarkson was living up to it. Was I living up to it? I didn't think so.

Resolutions

Through the youth fellowship, I found a book entitled *Martin Luther Had A Wife* by William Peterson. It was an interesting book about the marriage of some popular Fathers of the Christian faith, including Martin and Katie Luther, John and Molly Wesley, William and Catherine Booth, Dwight and Emma Moody, and Jonathan and Sarah Edwards. Edwards' marriage strongly impacted me, so I read further about him. I found out he had written something in his youth that has come down to us as *The Resolutions of Jonathan Edwards*. It is a series of seventy thoughts and practices that helped him grow in the Christian faith.

Once every week, he reviewed this list to remind himself what he was to live up to. These resolutions worked for Jonathan Edwards, who became a humble and Godly man whom God used to spark one of the greatest revivals known to history. Some of the key resolutions follow, beginning with:

Aware that I am unable to do anything without God's help, I do pray that, by his grace, he will enable me to keep these Resolutions, so far as they are in line with his will, and that they will honor Christ.

It continues:

Resolved: I will DO whatever I think will be most to God's glory and my own good, profit and pleasure for as long as I live. I will do all these things without any consideration of the time they take.

Resolved: To do whatever I understand to be my duty and will provide the most good and benefit to mankind in general. Resolved to do this, whatever difficulties I encounter, and no matter how many I experience or how severe they may be.

Resolved: I will continually endeavor to find new ways to practice and promote the things from Resolution 1.

Resolved: If ever—really, whenever—I fail and fall and/or grow weary and dull; whenever I begin to neglect the keeping of any part of these Resolutions, I will repent of everything I can remember that I have violated or neglected, ...as soon as I come to my senses again.

Resolved: Never to do anything, whether physically or spiritually, except what glorifies God. In fact, I resolve not only to this commitment, but I resolve not to even grieve and gripe about these things, ...if I can avoid it.

Resolved: Never lose one moment of time, but seize the time to use it in the most profitable way I possibly can.

I wanted to live this way, too. If only I could be a man like this. As I read this, I wondered if Jonathan Edwards was even a human like me. I wondered if he had the same struggles I did. I wondered if he faced the same challenges I faced. Gradually, I saw that Edwards was human after all; that was why he wrote down the resolutions and asked God to help him. He began with an acknowledgment of his frailty. Left on his own, he could not have achieved them.

Alas, that was the secret. To make a commitment and to submit it to God. That night before I went to bed, I wrote my resolutions, went on my knees, and asked God to make me a man like this. I hung the list close to my bed so I could see it every day. It stayed there until I had to move. It reminded me every day of the man I am supposed to be.

It was at this point that my panic monkey began undergoing some transformation. I had been an impulsive kid who dared whatever would be to get whatever he wanted. I took pride in this. My friends in school would often praise me for this. The more I encountered models of the Christian faith, the more I realized that there is a higher way of living. Perhaps my panic monkey could be turned into something much nobler, more respectable, and more useful for God. I began to hear friends in the fellowship say things like "That Lengdung guy, he is a thoughtful guy. He gives reasoned perspective from scriptures. I would love to have him in our Bible study group again." The previous Lengdung would have been very surprised at this comment.

Baptism Of Books

I returned home for an extended vacation break, which typically lasts from August to September. I had almost two months on my hands with nothing to do. I had grown apart from my previous friends in the community, and my new friends, like Peter, were busy working. My dad had this old stack of newspapers. He once worked at the Coca-Cola depot in Jos, where the company received weekly newspaper deliveries. One of these was the *Nigerian Standard*. He had been collecting that newspaper from the late 1970s till the most recent one of 2014. I began by reading the sports section out of boredom, which was very interesting for a football dreamer. But the sports page was often just two pages. I read through the sports pages in all the newspapers. After finishing, I realized there was nothing else to do, so I started reading other newspaper sections. Soon, I was reading from the first page to the last page. By the end of that holiday, I had read all the *Nigeria Standard* newspapers from the 1970s to 2014. My knowledge of Nigerian history swelled, and my understanding of Nigeria deepened. In one holiday, I went from almost no knowledge of Nigeria's history to being a pretty good commentator. It all started with boredom.

In SSS2, I came to my academic principal, Mr. Daniel Adisa, with a theological question. Our conversation left a deep impression on me about the power of reading.

"Sir, I have a question," I told him when I got to his house.

As usual, many students gathered around him, seeking solutions to their problems.

"Go ahead, Lengdung."

"Sir, if Jesus came only around 2,000 years ago, and there were millions of people who have lived before that, and there are many who didn't hear him before they died, how will they be judged?"

"Interesting question. Well, there are many responses to this. It is a question that has been asked across the ages by so many Christians. I would like to begin by asking you, how do you think they will be judged?"

"I don't know, Sir. That's why I am asking"

"Would you like to read about it? I have some books here I can share."

"Yes, Sir."

"You know, Lengdung, you have one great advantage over others:

you read. You will find all the answers you seek. You've caught on to one of the greatest tools of a good life, reading books."

Next to Grace, books became the greatest force that moved my life. They expanded my world, gave me a new imagination, and provided alternatives to life in Jenta. From then on, I would read something rather than hang out with idle friends.

JENTA READS

Another important aspect of Youth Fellowship was the caliber of people I connected with. These were the people who would play important roles in what I became and what happened to me. I connected with brilliant minds like Philip Dimka, Von Deme, and Clement Luka in the Youth Fellowship. Also, it was there that my friendship with Peter Kurdor was cemented. Although I was already friends with Peter, we bonded at the fellowship and shared our visions for life. All of this was done at the altar of God's word and a solid surrounding of influences ranging from Biblical figures to contemporary preachers. We were on the race to heaven, and we were traveling together. As it was popularly said, we were on fire. But our fire was different. We did not have the usual Pentecostal zeal for God. Each of us knew that our calling, or our vision, was not to be closed-circuited within the church. We were supposed to be in the world playing roles through which we would glorify God.

We were now confident that we could change the world, doing our part in making it a better place. We were not here to be another statistic. But before we could touch the globe, we first needed to become change agents in our own community, which has endless needs. Jenta is bedeviled with a lack of potable water, faces widespread teenage pregnancy, endures poverty like a quarrelsome next-door neighbor, and experiences perilously short lifespans. What could we do? We were just young men and women who were in school. We didn't have any political connections, nor did we have any money. We were all starting in life and had no networks to tap into. We were merely poor Jenta kids. But we still believed we could do something.

What was that something? What could we do? These are big problems that will at least involve the effort of many people and cost millions of Naira, if not dollars. Take the water problem, for instance; how can we connect water to a community of over 25,000 people? Do we connect pipes to every home, and even if we did that, who would pay the water bills? And assuming we get water in some period of the year, how about the other times when the government water board does not provide water? Finally, if we want to tackle the problem of poverty, how do we solve the problem of another's poverty when we are barely living from hand to mouth ourselves? These problems were bigger than us.

Our church had a long history of praying for the youths. Especially the mothers. They would often gather to pray and cry to God, saying, "God raise up the youths of Jenta to become useful kingdom ambassadors." They petitioned God on our behalf, praying that He would guide us and help us avoid the ways of the world. I have heard these prayers for years since I was a kid. Faithfully, year after year, they offered their heart cries to God, during weekly service, midweek prayers, and night vigils. They believed with all their hearts that God was listening. They knew it would happen. There was no doubt about it in their minds. Sometimes, listening to them, I would walk out of the church believing it, too. It was as though, as I walked out of the church, I was already walking into a new reality. A popular passage they used during those prayers was Joel 2:28.

"It will come about after this, That I will pour out My Spirit on all mankind; And your sons and your daughters will prophesy, Your old men will have dreams, Your young men will see visions."

Sometimes, during those prayers, mothers would hold the hands of youths in the church and make declarations upon their lives. They were all positive declarations. In their voices, you could hear the hopes and dreams they had for us. You could hear their desperation. We were their last hope. Life had been tough for them, and they wanted us to have a better life.

We are sons of prayer. Those prayers made us.

Now, it was our turn to carry it forward.

Yet, we kept praying and saying, "God, we are here. You've sent us here for a purpose. How can we be ambassadors of your kingdom in Jenta?" We prayed and prayed, for there was nothing else we could do. More importantly, we believed. We believed that, indeed, God would use us. In our hearts, we could feel the sense of the calling. We just didn't know what it was.

On July 4th, 2017, the answer came.

Philip Dimka had gone to a July 4th event at the American Corner in Jos City. It was an event to celebrate Independence Day in America. As the program went on, the quote by John F. Kennedy appeared on the screen: "Ask not what your country can do for you, but ask what you can do for your country." The speakers at the event inspired the attendees to do something for their community. No matter how little. As he sat there, he wrote on Facebook, "I am starting a local library in my community, Jenta. Who will be part of this? Who will pray along and support?"

Within minutes, I responded that this was the call. This was the task. Peter Kurdor also added his voice. As the day went by and we shared the post, we began to use the hashtag #ChangingTheNarrative. For us, this was the call to change the negative narrative of Jenta. After a day of sharing and resharing, it became clear that we were merely talking online. The real work needed to begin. We called for a meeting with other youths within the community. We met at COCIN Jenta Mangoro, the church where we met for the youth fellowship and prayer meetings. We shared the vision for what we needed to do and how to do it. Inspired by the online conversations and the meeting, we named our new efforts Jenta Reads Community Initiative.

Deciding to do something for our community and giving it a name did not guarantee its success. Organizing meetings and meeting other potential stakeholders within the community did not guarantee success either. To follow through with our vision, we planned to visit every major church and every community leader. We would see a church and request a meeting with the pastor. The pastor would give us an audience, and we would ask for the opportunity to address the church youths. Our pitch usually went like this:

"We all know the problems in Jenta. We've waited for the government for many years, but the government has done nothing. We can either keep waiting or try to do something. We've watched our finest men and women waste their lives in this jungle, and we will continue to witness this unless something changes. And together, we can change something. We are starting this community library, which will become a hub for change in Jenta. It will provide a place for young people to visit. Instead of going to the jungle, they will go to the library. School-goers will have access to the library, entrepreneurs will have access to the library, and just about anyone will have access to the library. It will be a theatre of dreams. Come and join us to make a difference. Donate your books or anything you have. Posterity will be kind to you."

In most cases, the pitch succeeded in that the pastor would tell us how excited he was to hear about this new initiative and how he had long wanted to make a difference, too. He would promise to get back to us in a few days. To this day, we have never heard from any of them. In many churches, the actual reception happened amongst the young people. The youths, whose futures were at stake, were more open to our message. After delivering a talk at ECWA Church Jenta Mangoro, Ogbole Peter, a youth from the church, called to say he had some old books from his secondary school days. A young lady, Esther Fatsen, called some days later to say she had some books to donate. While doing physical outreach, we also used our Facebook profiles to solicit for books. It was not uncommon to see up to five posts in a day requesting used books or materials. We received donations from other neighborhoods: Tudun Wada, Gada Biu, Angwan Rukuba, and Rukuba Road. These communities faced the same problems as Jenta, yet their residents felt inspired by our appeals.

Soon, we had a new problem: we had received some books, and now people were asking if they could borrow books. Philip Dimka had his own room in his grandmother's house, and I also had a room, so we opened our bedrooms to the public, turning them into libraries. Anyone who wanted a book would visit one of our houses and get the books they wanted. Borrowing books was something utterly new in the community. Students in Jenta, especially those whose parents could not afford textbooks and whose schools didn't have libraries, found our little initiative most helpful. They would visit us daily, borrow, and return to borrow again. The limitation of such a service was obvious: they could not stay in our rooms and read, and they didn't have a conducive study environment at home. We started to tinker with solutions. Would anyone in the community lend us a property for free to use for a library? We asked around and visited prominent people in the community to seek help. None came.

Simultaneously, we realized we could address a different problem—the problem of water. The government water board could supply water via trucks to specific individuals who could then sell the water to community members at a profit. We negotiated with the truck owners to sell at a reasonable rate, and in turn, we could sell to the community members at a reduced rate. They agreed, and soon after, we started supplying water to the community. We would haul the water in wheelbarrows house by house. We kept a daily record of the water provided. Within one month, we had supplied 1,000 jerrycans of water. Supplying water allowed us to create awareness about Jenta Reads and what we were trying to achieve. Although we did not get any concrete response, it created trust in the hearts of community members. And since we could do menial jobs such as water delivery at a reasonable rate, they were willing to embrace our vision. Many months later, the trust we built during this time became an essential factor in the sustainability of our initiative. However, the money from selling water was barely enough to sustain the water supply efforts and not enough to feed us for a single day.

What else could we do besides the library that would not cost us money? Seminars? Workshops? We had another brainstorming session. These sessions were a combination of prayer, thinking, and talking. We organized a seminar on financial discipline. The free event sought young people who were not making enough. Although we were not rich, we knew from studies that the basic building blocks of wealth building included things such as saving and avoiding lifestyle creep, among others. We could teach this to each other and anyone who wanted to come around. There would also be light refreshments. Food was a great attraction in a community where many members go to bed on empty stomachs. The day arrived, and we met in a small classroom at COCIN Church Jenta Mangoro. We had a lively conversation and teaching. Afterward, we had our refreshments, took photos, and headed home.

Now that we'd learned how to build wealth, could we use some of that wealth to begin a physical venue for Jenta Reads? The joke was on us. There was still no money. We couldn't afford a physical space for Jenta Reads. At this point, the reality of our efforts began to weigh on us. Did we really think we could establish a community library here? Where did we expect the money for such an effort to come from? We were sure everyone in the community would be enthusiastic and happy to collaborate somehow. We were terribly mistaken. While some community members embraced the idea, none was willing to put his money behind it. Our enthusiasm was fading. I, for one, began to question God.

"God, do you really want us to do this? I think so. And yet you haven't provided for our needs? How can we proceed with nothing?"

I asked the team if we knew this was God's calling. But while the doubts were there, the vision was stronger. We would follow the vision. Or perhaps it wasn't the vision but the desire for something new, fueled by a hatred for the old life of indifference, mediocrity, suffering, and the same cycle of poverty. We just wanted to try something new that might lift even a few people, starting with ourselves, out of the Jenta mindset.

We decided to go around the community again to seek a loan. We visited two well-established men in the community. The first man told us about the futility of borrowing to start a library that would not generate any revenue. How would we sustain it after the first year, assuming we could pay his loan? We had no answer. The second man we visited was Mr. Justin, an accountant who had a reputation for being a principled man and a lover of books, a reputation he lived up to. He told us, "See, the truth is, things are difficult, and it would be hard to loan you the amount you seek. However, I have a small room that has become my personal library. It was supposed to be my store, but it has turned into a personal study. If you are interested, I could lend it to you to use for the Jenta Reads Community Library."

Incredible!

That became the door that opened all other doors. It was a small room that could seat at most three people at the same time. It had a narrow hole that served as a window and a doorway so short that I had to stoop to get in, but it was a space—a space we could use for our library. Over the next few weeks, we moved the books from our homes to our new space and began creating awareness about the new location. We were also still soliciting book donations on social media.

The most significant support came from those living outside the Jenta community. A friend from Lagos sent some books. A mentor from Kaduna sent his collections. A Facebook acquaintance also sent his old books. Little by little, we were getting these donations, and they were making a difference. Although the library space was small enough only to allow three people at a time, it was a good place for borrowing. Community members were trooping in every day to borrow. Friends from social media were also visiting out of curiosity to see this new library space. It was fascinating because they never would have believed that Jenta would have a library. Children were the most frequent visitors. They would come in search of textbooks and ask for help with their assignments, as some of them came from families that didn't value education. At the library, they received the help they sought. A popular shop owner came to borrow a book by Robert Kiyosaki. He attended a seminar that recommended the book. Thus, they came. The business owners, the school children, the school dropouts, and any community member who wanted to read. Within a few months, we had outgrown the space.

At this point, we had a proof of concept. It was evident that this would make a big difference in our community. However, we stalled again. We needed to expand, but there was no way. We told ourselves we would pray and wait it out. The pace of our outreach never slackened. Every weekend, we organized presentations to people we thought could help.

CHAPTER 14

AN UNLIKELY FRIENDSHIP

The human mind is like the lake behind a dam, and reading is like the water poured into it. The more you read, the more you fill the lake. Eventually, it comes to a point where the dam bursts and the flood of ideas pours out, which seems to be the case for the great writers I've encountered. This was also my story. Having read so many books, I wanted to express myself. Beginning in secondary school, I kept diaries, a book of quotes, and a book of letters. I wrote countless letters.

In 2017, I started writing letters to C. S. Lewis, the writer who influenced me more than any other. I had to find a way to express the profound effect Lewis' writings had on me. A typical letter would begin, "Dear Uncle Lewis, thank you for writing the book..." Through these letters, I could work out my thoughts and express to others the things I had learned from his books.

The most influential of Lewis' books were the seven Chronicles of Narnia, which greatly blessed me and opened my imagination to another world. At that time, I would rather live in Narnia than in Jenta.

My mum had a wardrobe for her clothes, and when she died, I inherited it. As a male, it was the only thing I could inherit from her, since her clothes and accessories were mostly female in nature. The wardrobe gained even more meaning when I learned that the Narnia story began when four children, Peter, Susan, Edmond, and Lucy, entered the fantasy land through the wardrobe of old Professor Kirke. Now, my mother's wardrobe allowed my imagination to expand. In those days, I felt deeply refreshed by mentally immersing myself in the stories of the four children, never imagining that my own story could be just as exciting.

Over time, the wardrobe became my bookshelf. I kept the few books I had collected in it. Yes, I was aware that wardrobes are supposed to be for clothes. But this particular wardrobe had been sanctified by the imaginative memory it had for me related to books. Therefore, its highest purpose was fulfilled by being a bookshelf. At the same time, I didn't have another option as I could not afford a bookshelf.

I initiated my bookshelf with my brand new copy of *Mere Christianity*. On getting home after purchasing the book, I placed it in the wardrobe and just smiled at it! Mission accomplished. My C. S. Lewis fantasy world was taking shape. That day, I felt as though I had achieved something extraordinary. I suspect C. S. Lewis would have been proud of me. Yes, I did not have all his books, just one. And I did not even have a small library of books. But on that specific day, I had done all I could to obtain my first copy of a C. S. Lewis work, and now it was in my special wardrobe. That was all that mattered.

Lewis was such a significant influence on me that I was trying to bring his imaginative world into my real world. I spent more time in Narnia than in Jenta. It was an escape from the constant reality of the chaos I had to endure every day.

C. S. Lewis was a man who sought to incorporate spiritual matters into every area of life. I also admired his unconventional attitude. I liked the fact that his writings were simple and exploratory. Lewis wrote as though he was not pointing to a thing; he wanted the reader to find out for himself what was there. Through carefully crafted questions, he made absolute claims without dogmatically insisting they were absolute claims. I had read all seven of the Chronicles of Narnia before knowing it was a Christian story featuring Aslan as Jesus. I admired the loyalty of some of the animals and celebrated the bravery of some of the school children, their forgiveness, the sacrifice of Aslan, and the ultimate triumph that good will always win. Not until much later did I see that Narnia presented a picture of the Christian life.

When I started writing the "Letters to Uncle Lewis," I posted them on Facebook in the previously mentioned group "C. S. Lewis and His Master." This group focused on the works of C. S. Lewis and his literary "master," George MacDonald, a nineteenth-century author who profoundly influenced C. S. Lewis. David Jack, a Scottish publisher of George MacDonald's works, created the group. It comprised people from many different countries, including a few Nigerians. The Letters became popular in the group. I received hundreds of reactions, several good comments, and some friend requests.

One such friend request was from an American named Thaine Norris. At first, we were just Facebook friends without any conversation until I posted a status update that said, "Do you want to grow fast? Read books and walk with grown-ups." Thaine commented, asking if I had read a particular book, *The Heavenly Man,* by Brother Yun. I replied in the negative. He recommended that I should. Several weeks later, he asked if I had read it yet, and I said no. At this point, he was curious about why, so I was honest with him, telling him I couldn't find the book in Nigeria, as getting specific books was difficult and even getting books, in general, could be a challenge. He immediately offered to purchase an ebook copy and send it to me if I promised to read it. I readily agreed. He sent it, and I read the book gradually. When I finished, I realized it had become a profound blessing. When we discussed it, I informed Thaine that I had written another letter, a "Letter to Uncle Yun." That was when he told me he could get the letter to Brother Yun because he worked with Back To Jerusalem, the ministry under which Brother Yun works. Wow.

And thus began an unlikely friendship.

Thaine and I met in a C. S. Lewis group. This author, whom we both loved, had become the middle ground upon which a friendship could begin. C. S. Lewis had written many years ago, "Friendship… is born at the moment when one man says to another 'What! You, too? I thought that no one but myself…'"

Our "You, too" was C. S. Lewis himself.

Thaine was in his fifties and described himself simply as "a follower of Jesus." He was born into a non-religious family, but Christ found him as a teenager. He had a long career as a computer programmer, although he would say that his "full-time job" was being a missionary because he would say that being a missionary is simply the normal Christian life. Thaine was not the kind of missionary I was familiar with in Nigeria. Instead of working full-time for some huge missionary-sending organization, he sought to fill his life with Jesus and share that fullness with others through life's "normal" activities. But even what he called normal life activities took him all over the world in ministry. His lovely wife, Erika, shared the same passions, and he liked to describe her as his "better half." I know this to be true.

On the other hand, I was just a twenty-year-old kid from Nigeria. Thaine had kids my age. What could we have in common? First, we both enjoyed reading C. S. Lewis and other books. Second, we shared a passion for Jesus. And we had a few more things in common, like computers, which were enough to build a friendship, a discipleship, and a father-son relationship that has changed my life.

As I've said, my father had not played a very active role in my childhood. He did his best, given what he knew and what he had, but a young man needs a mentor. Thaine would play that role in more ways than I could have prayed for.

Our shared passion for books provided fodder for numerous conversations. I would read a book and rush to Thaine,

"Have you read this?"

"No. What is it about?"

"Ah. You must read this! It's about…"

Thaine would read my book recommendation and be blessed as well. Another time, it would be Thaine sharing his most recent read.

One time, I read *God's Smuggler* by Brother Andrew and came to Thaine with the exciting announcement as usual. "Have you read God's Smuggler? Oh my, this is too good."

"Yes. Yes, I've read this! It's a Christian classic!"

"Wait, you did? Why didn't you tell me about it? This is a must-read that I should have read years ago."

And on and on it went. Conversations on books, walking with Jesus, US politics, Nigeria, our families, and what was happening in our lives.

At this time, my father remarried. Family tensions rose for me and my sisters due to the strain of living with a stepmother. As the sole male child expected to lead, I was caught between feuding factions. During my lowest moments, I confided in Thaine, who offered understanding and directed me to the Bible for perspective. His non-judgmental listening and simple guidance to pray and emulate Jesus provided the clarity I needed to make better choices and grow in faith. Thaine, a true caring friend, respected my autonomy and consistently reminded me to maintain a simple faith in Jesus.

The more comfortable our friendship became, the more I shared with him, and the more he shared his life with me. I was more likely to inform him of anything happening in my life than I was to share with my biological father. Soon, I made the distinction. Thaine was "Dad," and my biological father was "Father."

But Thaine was not just a dad. He was a friend. While we have met in person at least once a year since we first became friends, Thaine was a friend who was constantly present digitally. I felt his guidance more than many people I knew physically. I would tell him about the ladies I liked, the temptation to get a girlfriend, and my thoughts about the future. He would ask, "What would a girlfriend do for you at this point?" Such questions made me rethink. Other times, he would tell me stories about how he and Erika met and got married. He would encourage me that the best way to find a fitting wife was to do my calling and walk with Jesus. In the process, I would find my soulmate. It was not a result of some strategizing and intense "search for the missing rib."

Whenever Thaine said, "I will pray for you," I knew he would pray for me.

A central theme for our conversation was "the kingdom lifestyle." How does God expect us to live on earth? How does God expect us to live with our neighbors, friends, and families? Will this please God? We often talked about how something should be done according to the way of the Kingdom of God rather than according to the African way or the American way. Many centuries ago, Paul wrote to the Corinthians, "Therefore, we are ambassadors for Christ, God making his appeal through us." This applied to us, too. How could we live this out? Thaine was my constant discussion partner when exploring these questions.

In October of 2017, there was another attack by Fulani herdsmen in Bassa Local Government Area (LGA) in Plateau State. The attack killed over thirty people, burned houses, and displaced thousands. This was just one in a series of attacks that became a common feature of Plateau State to this day.

The whole state erupted in anger—anger at the security forces for failing to provide safety despite an army barracks located in the same LGA and anger at the state government for refusing to safeguard lives and property. I was also angry at God. How could he allow this?

Many people, including me, demanded revenge. Left to us, it was an easy thing. Each time there was an attack like that, the Christians would respond by getting weapons and attacking the Fulani Muslim communities nearby. Simple.

As I expressed these feelings to Thaine and published them on Facebook, we began conversing about what a Kingdom of God response would be. Thaine pointed out that Jesus commands us to do hard things, such as loving our enemies and laying down our rights. But Jesus does not command us to lay down our neighbor's rights. They are not ours to give. Jesus commands Christians to love their neighbors, so we must defend their rights. We must seek justice for those suffering injustice.

These online discussions made me think deeply about government and what I should expect in a sane society. I took a government course in secondary school for three months but did not think about it deeply. Thaine was leading me to do that and to do it biblically. Through his questions and his prodding, I realized that it was not revenge I needed; it was not revenge that Nigeria needed. It was justice. These were new thoughts, contrary to everything I was raised to believe. I had always thought that the reason the Christians in Jos were victims of these attacks was because they were slow to arm themselves and to take revenge whenever attacked. Of course, I never took it to heart that Muslims have also been victims of attacks in Plateau State and Nigeria as a whole. Both Christians and Muslims have been victims. They were ordinary citizens failed by a government whose primary duty was to protect lives and property. A functional government seeking justice is the God-ordained tool that ensures that law-abiding citizens are safe and criminals are punished.

I would remind Thaine that we don't have a functional government in Nigeria, and he would say there is only one ideal government. The Kingdom of God is a society where loving one's neighbor is the governing principle. And there is only one way to establish that perfect government: individually submit to King Jesus and begin to love our neighbors, one at a time. Jesus said this would add up and multiply like yeast until it fills the earth. Thaine constantly talks about the Parable of the Yeast.

My thinking entered a new phase. Thaine had directed me here. He guided me in other ways, too. For instance, in 2019, Anita Clarkson encouraged me to consider formal theological training, considering all my conversations with her. Thaine simply asked me, "What do you hope to achieve with formal theological training?" I didn't know; hence, I didn't sign up.

While I read books that showed me Christian heroes and mentors, Thaine became my real-life Christian hero. He was not just preaching about Jesus; he was trying to live like him. Yet he would be the first to admit his failures, which endeared him to me more. I could not meet C. S. Lewis on this side of Heaven, but I could have a deep friendship with another "fellow Narnian" who had more experience, more wisdom, and more passion for Jesus than I did. And I was flattered that an older man, an American, would genuinely listen to my thoughts and talk to me like an adult.

I still say that our friendship has been the biggest miracle of my life. What were the odds that a Nigerian youth could meet a middle-aged American man—on Facebook, of all places—and that they would become true friends and trust each other? Nigerians had a reputation for Yahoo yahoo, but this man saw beyond that and trusted me with the gift of friendship. The odds were slim, but God made it happen. ("Yahoo yahoo" is a Nigerian slang term that refers to Internet fraud, "Yahoo" referring to the popular Internet company, and "yahoo" meaning "up to no good.")

CHAPTER 15

My Friend is Coming to Nigeria

While the Jenta Reads team was "praying and waiting it out," thousands of miles away in America, Thaine was praying something different. He was praying and asking, "God, what are you doing that I can be a part of?" On most days, according to him, the answer to this prayer was simply, "Get up off your knees and wash the dishes." But once, the Lord impressed upon him to look more closely at Jenta Reads, which he and his wife had been following on Facebook. In our online conversation one day, he asked, "What's the address to send some books if I wanted to send books to you?"

"Our postal service hardly works, but here it is."

Some weeks later, Thaine went to a local shipping office to send his thirty-three-pound box of books to Nigeria. He was shocked when they said,

"The cost to send these books to Nigeria is $830."

"$830?!?"

"Yes."

Thaine did not ship the box. Instead, he returned to his house, wondering how much it would cost to go to Nigeria himself. A quick search revealed that a flight to Nigeria cost about $930. He sent me a message saying he is increasingly considering coming to Nigeria.

"Does Jos have an international airport? What's the nearest airport to Jos?"

"Enugu."

"But from what I can see, Abuja is closer to Jos than Enugu."

I just gave the first place that entered my mind because I had not taken his question seriously. I could not believe that he was determined enough to want to bring the books to Nigeria. I had not known this man before; I had never met him, and I had never done anything worthy of his trust. I was deeply conscious of the reputation that Nigerians had over the Internet. There was no chance he would trust a Nigerian on this.

Nevertheless, Thaine pressed on. In the spring of 2018, he sent a message saying that his heart was in the Jenta Reads project and that he would like to bring us books. What? This was crazy! I could not believe he was still talking about it. Then Thaine messaged,

> *"Erika and I were so excited for me to deliver books to Jenta Reads. But as we thought about it more, and as we searched the Internet for information about Nigeria, we began to wonder if it was really a good idea. So we prayed and asked God, 'Lord if this is of You, would you provide the funds for travel outside of our income? As confirmation of Your will?' We then went away for a week to visit Erika's parents. Upon our return we saw the pile of mail our neighbors had collected for us. On top of the stack was an envelope from a ministry we have donated to and volunteered for, and in the envelope was a handwritten check for $1,000. What was this? This is the wrong direction for donations to flow! I called the office to ask the reason, and the person responsible said, 'No reason, I just felt led by the Lord to send you this money.' Well, there is the answer, clear as day. Praise God!"*

Now, it was real. Thaine could come to Nigeria. He had mentioned that he didn't want to stay in the hotel. He wanted to stay in our home to get to know me, my family and the whole Jenta Reads team better. I had to inform my dad. But first, I told the Jenta Reads team about our communications with Thaine and the plans for a visit. Some believed; others did not. However, Philip, Peter, and Shedrack Deshi were fully on board, and we began to ask questions and plan how to make the visit possible.

After evening prayers, I told my dad to kindly wait as I had something important to say. This is often how we initiate conversations about our needs and important things to our father.

"Father, there is an American friend I met online. He is a missionary and computer programmer. We met on Facebook and talked about books for several months. He has seen what we are doing with Jenta Reads and has said he wants to visit us. He will be arriving in Nigeria in May and would like to stay at our home."

My dad stood up and left me sitting there.

The next day, I went to tell the news to my distant Aunty, Mrs. Gotus, and to report how my father treated me. She told me in a calm and kindly voice, "You know, you need to have some respect and treat elders with their due respect. Of course, this nonsense you are saying deserves no hearing. It is why your father left you. If you tell this lie to others, at least don't tell it to your dad."

I now understood better. I sounded like a madman who didn't deserve any hearing. Who was I to tell him that I had made friends on Facebook with a white man who wanted to visit me? I tried to make my case to my aunty to explain the relationship with Thaine, our conversations, and our level of trust in each other. She would hear none of it. She finished by saying, "You know, that's how scammers do it. At best, he would be a scammer who would get your money and go. He is most likely a Nigerian from the Southeast who is just trying to get you to commit money. Then he will disappear." I tried to explain to her that Thaine had never asked for money. We've never had any conversation related to me sending money to him. To her, the fact that the "scammer" hadn't asked for money was further proof of his scheme to ask for money at the very end.

When I realized I was trying to explain myself to an inconvincible personality, I thanked her for her time and left. The next visit was to the prospective house where we thought Thaine could stay. After some brainstorming with Philip, we decided the house of the Gomas was the best place. The Gomas were a princely family of the Ngas tribe. They had a large compound often used for tribal meetings and seasonal celebrations. They had extra rooms that could serve well. And there was Zingit, the last born of the family, who could help with meals and other household needs. Thaine would have everything to make his stay comfortable: his own room, meals, and a very clean pit latrine, the most common toilet available. Many houses in the community didn't have any toilets at all, and so the people used the rocks for open defecation. For us, Thaine's visit would be the first realization that many of these things are uncommon in other parts of the world, exposing us to our poverty.

We couldn't just assume that we could use the Goma's house. We had to ask Mama Goma, a widow with two children living with her at the time. She was one of the mothers within Jenta that made the community come alive, along with my mother. Mr. Goma was the King of the Ngas in Jos town. He had died almost a decade before.

Philip and I were assigned to talk to Mama Goma and request permission for Thaine to stay at her place. We visited her one evening and detailed the situation. Mama Goma was the first adult who believed us. Not only that, she became enthusiastic and got involved in all the other planning. An elderly friend in Jenta advised us to do our best to make Thaine's visit as comfortable as possible, even though we didn't have much. He told us that Thaine would return to the US and give testimony about his visit; therefore, we couldn't afford to be shabby about it.

For his part, Thaine had been researching on the Internet about Nigeria, particularly Jos. The results were not encouraging. The top ten search results showed headlines of violent crises and other negative things about the city. Thaine was no stranger to such experiences. His family had served as missionaries in one of the most dangerous cities on the US/Mexico border. Accustomed to violence, he also understood that news reports often exaggerate the reality on the ground. Having never met a Nigerian before, he searched the Internet for someone who lived in Jos and who could provide a more objective picture than what the sensational news paints. Thaine found a missionary couple, Bob and Meredith DeVoe, who had lived in Jos for many years and assured him it was a safe place to visit. Thus began the connection with a wonderful couple who would tremendously impact the work at Jenta Reads.

The DeVoes arrived in Nigeria in the early 2000s to begin missionary work. After nearly two decades of living in Nigeria, they had turned Nigerian except in skin color. Thaine had also asked Bob to check with us and verify that everything he'd learned about a library in the middle of a slum was true. And from our perspective, we wanted to make sure Bob was not the know-it-all type of missionary. The know-it-all type would have strong ideas of how he thought we should go about such a project. For that kind of person, it wouldn't matter what our ideas were, what our convictions were, or how God was leading us.

We linked up with Bob, and our first encounter dissolved all our fears. He told us, "Hello, everyone. My Name is Robert DeVoe. I am a Reverend with ECWA, but there is no need to call me 'Reverend.' You can call me Bob. I became a Reverend after I realized that Nigerians value titles, and if a title was the way to reach these people, why not?" Bob is still one of the most entertaining men I've ever known. You meet him for the first time, and he wins you with sincerity, passion, and infectious laughter.

For the final logistics, Bob connected us with a driver who knew how to navigate Nigerian roads safely. I had never traveled to Abuja before. Oh yes, and this was the time in which kidnappings on the highway were common.

Step by step, everything was falling in line.

On May 2nd, 2018, I left home for Abuja to pick up Thaine from the Nnamdi Azikiwe International Airport. His flight was arriving by 4:30 p.m. Our journey time from Jos to Abuja was about four hours. It was enough time to think about everything. Would Thaine really come to Nigeria? What if he didn't come? What would I tell all those back home that didn't believe me? Well, what if he did arrive? How would I welcome him? Would he be comfortable living in Jenta, with our poverty-stricken life? Would he be safe?

At around 5 p.m., I received a call from a Nigerian number. The voice on the other end said, "Hello. This is Thaine Norris. Am I speaking to Lengdung Tungchamma?"

"Yes. This is Lengdung. Hi, Thaine."

"I am at the airport already. Where are you?"

"I am at the gate. Give us a few minutes. We will be with you."

We were late for pickup. Thaine was there already. Were we starting Thaine's arrival with problems? Would this end well?

We were at the pickup point a few minutes later, and I could see Thaine. He saw us driving through and started walking towards us. When we finally met, he hugged me so tightly that all the tension and all the stress washed away in a moment. When we got back into the car to drive to our hotel, the driver looked at me and asked,

"You told me you've never met this man before, and you said you didn't know him until now. Look at the way you hugged each other. Are you lying to me?"

I couldn't find words to explain. It was a friendship already deeply rooted in conversations around books, stories, and God.

We stayed at a Catholic mission hotel that night. We spent the whole evening talking about our heroes. We talked in the dining room, and when we returned to our rooms, we sat on the stairs to talk even more. It was a continuation of a relationship, not an introduction, even though we had never before met in person. We picked up right where we left off in our online conversations.

When we got to Jos, the entire Jenta Reads team and the whole family were waiting for us at Mama Goma's house. After some hours of rest, we rushed to the library space at Mr. Justin's house. Thaine couldn't wait to show us the books he had for us, some of which we had selected ourselves, and we couldn't wait to see them. Some books we had sought all our lives, and some were no longer in print; most were impossible to get in Nigeria. Now, Thaine had brought them. Why wait?

"Oh, is that C. S. Lewis? Is that The Chronicles of Narnia?"

I said this after seeing The Chronicles of Narnia for the first time in print. I had read them in eBooks only.

"Oh! And that is George MacDonald. Dear George MacDonald," and Philip practically hugged the book. It was a book he had sought for years.

"G. K. Chesterton!" another person exclaimed when *The Everlasting Man* was pulled from the box.

We were like kids in a well-stocked candy shop. We had books, hard-to-find books—books we had never seen in print, and some new books. Although Thaine delivered books for Jenta Reads on that first visit, in retrospect, the books were only a minor part of what he brought. His very visit was the biggest blessing of all. For the first time, our community members began to listen to us. During his visit, we went around Jenta, introducing him to local community leaders and church leaders. Community members began to wonder, "What is in books after all? What is so important about Jenta Reads that a white man would leave his home and visit Nigeria just to visit these boys and girls who have no worldly influence whatsoever?" His presence convinced the community that whatever was happening here must be important. It was the most significant PR we ever received, and it turned everything around. All of a sudden, those we had sought were now seeking us. If not for anything, just so they could take a photo with the white man and tell him about how they supported reading.

For his part, Thaine wanted to meet everyone. Before he arrived in Nigeria, he told me, "I want to meet your community, your mentors, and those who prayed for you. I want to meet the people that helped form you as a person, because they must be amazing people!" We did. Together with Philip Dimka, Peter Kurdor, Deshi Shedrach, and the rest of the Jenta Reads team, we met as many of my mentors as possible. We visited Peter Emmanuel and saw his personal library. We traveled to Bokkos to visit All Nations Academy and the principal, Daniel Adisa. We went house to house to greet the many "praying aunties." We had American-style fast food with Bob DeVoe in central Jos. We met the Youth Fellowship, did radio interviews, visited leadership mentors and many others. Sadly, Anita Clarkson had moved away before Thaine's visit, but still, he could appreciate the vast network of people God had put into my life.

This visit, and many others in the years to come, provided us with opportunities to really know each other, hear each other's laughter, mock each other's accents, snap countless photos, eat many Nigerian dishes, and talk about so many things in person. Our online friendship blossomed into a beautiful face-to-face friendship. It was as though we had known each other for many years.

Up NEPA!

Now that Thaine was here, there was some "getting to know Nigeria" that he needed to go through, such as the fact that electricity is not a constant. He would hear us exclaim, "Up NEPA!" whenever the power came on. At first, Thaine found this surprising. He came from a world of continuous electricity, where an outage was rare. As the days passed, he soon joined in our excitement whenever the light was restored. "Up NEPA" was now slang he could adopt since his phone battery was often at the red bar.

NEPA is supposed to mean National Electric Power Authority, but due to their failures, they've been christened "Never Expect Power Always." Power failure is a regular part of the Nigerian experience. It is not uncommon for the entire nationwide electrical grid to collapse, plunging nearly two hundred million people into darkness. Even when the grid is working, power is still rationed according to economic status. Wealthier neighborhoods of Jos may have power almost continuously, but some days in Jenta, we get two hours of light supply, and other days, we get none. It is possible to go months without electricity. One time in Jenta, we went six months without electricity until the community raised enough money to pay a bribe to some middle-man.

One time, I was on a flight from Abuja to Egypt. As usual, the pilot turned off the cabin lights for take-off. When the pilot turned the lights back on after we were in the air, a little boy on the plane shouted, "Up NEPA!" The whole plane, all Nigerians, burst out laughing. We could all relate to the "Up NEPA" phenomenon, a Nigerian thing. It has been a campaign subject for Nigerian politicians since the 1960s; every politician promises to end the "Up NEPA" phenomenon. My grandfather was promised the same thing, my father was promised the same thing, and today's politicians have promised me the same thing. When will it end? No one can say.

To Inculcate a Reading Culture

Together with Thaine, we visited about a dozen schools within Jos, preaching the gospel of reading. Thaine's wife, Erika, had written an essay for Jenta Reads about the benefits of reading, and Thaine adapted it for speaking. Through reading, one can travel through time, space, and imagination, get to know amazing people, and even learn skills. And then the most significant benefit of becoming a reader is knowing God in His Word. The Jenta Reads team would follow and steal the show with compelling stories from popular figures such as Ben Carson, Abraham Lincoln, Helen Keller, Frederick Douglass, etc. At the end of the presentation, we would have a question-and-answer session. In a typical scene, a boy would raise his hand and say,

"Good afternoon, Sir. Thank you so much for coming to our school. I am inspired to read and become like all the great people you mentioned, but where can I get the books to read?"

Our standard response was always that they could visit the Jenta Reads library, which was open to everyone in the public. However, some of these schools were kilometers away, and the possibility of students between twelve and eighteen moving that far to get books at Jenta Reads Community Library was near zero. The standard answer we gave was just a standard answer. It didn't solve the problem. As we visited more schools over time, it became clear that we couldn't ignore this request. If we wanted students to read, we had to do something else. This question dominated our minds for years. How do we make Jenta Reads available to those outside Jenta?

Meanwhile, Thaine's visit was going well. We were getting to know each other better. We prayed together, ate together, worked together, and talked about books books books. It was the first time I realized I talk too fast and type almost as fast. In conversations, Thaine would say, "Slow down so I can hear you."

Like all good things, Thaine's trip was coming to an end. May 9th came too fast. We were all in tears. A good time had come to an end.

Although Thaine had come to visit us, the reality was that our physical needs had not improved. We still did not have a proper library. We were still trusting God for answers. An answer came in a surprising way. What's more surprising is that we had to refuse it.

CHAPTER 16

THE POLITICIAN

I have a friend who, in 2018, was a politician contesting for the role of Governor of Plateau State. We visited his campaign office in Jos on Thaine's second day in Nigeria. A few days later, my friend and his team visited Jenta for the first time to visit the library. Many carefully staged photographs were taken, including one with many children and the white guy.

But the most fantastic thing about the visit was what didn't happen. We all went to visit the tiny library at Mr. Justin's. My friend struggled to get in, for he was a huge man. With all his media team, it was a big show. Once packed in, my friend said, "This place is too small. Tomorrow I will come back to Jenta and we will find a three-room house to rent for the library. With this, you can start to expand. We will do this tomorrow, and I will pay for it." Thaine seemed excited as he listened. But I knew this was not a good idea. When my friend finished, I respectfully said, "Thank you very much for your kind offer, but we have to decline. We believe God has something for us, and we will trust Him for it." After the visit, as we were all walking back to

Mama Goma's, Thaine was surprised by my response. He said, "What was that all about? Why did you turn down his offer?"

The day before the politician's visit, the Jenta Reads team gathered under the mango tree at Mama Goma's. I told Thaine that we would have a business meeting and that he should take the opportunity to rest as he was still feeling the effects of jet lag. We had been a praying team since Jenta Reads had grown out of the Youth Fellowship. Prayer is how we conduct our business. One of the resolutions born out of prayer that day was that the library should have no political affiliations. Instead, we resolved to trust God to provide the perfect place and to meet all the library's needs. My friend's gift was well-intentioned and indeed could have hastened all our plans. However, it would also mean we were giving a politician the library. We would be giving our loyalty to him. Politics in Nigeria is dependent on give and take. Once a politician gives you something, he takes your loyalty and dignity in exchange. You must praise his candidacy, support him even when he is wrong, and defend him from his critics. We were not interested in that.

My panic monkey instinct had been tamed; from impulse to initiative, from grasping to patient faith. Now, I could take risks for things God had laid in my heart, like joining my friends to start Jenta Reads, and I could say no to things that God had clearly warned against.

To an outside observer, as it was to Thaine at the moment, it was absurd to turn down such a generous offer. But God had prepared me ahead of time to respond in faith. And God didn't make us wait very long. A few weeks after we turned down the politician's offer, we received an email that read:

> *Dear Applicant,*
> *It is my pleasure to inform you that your team has been selected as one of the three finalists to pitch at the 4th edition of the Emerging Leaders Award Programme. The event is scheduled to take place as follows:*

Date: July 14th, 2018
Venue: Details will be communicated in due course
Time: 11:00 a.m.

Please be informed that at this stage, we would only require a member to represent you all at the finalist pitch.

In the meantime, please acknowledge receipt of this email and do not hesitate to contact me directly at [email address] should you require any further information.

Accept our profound Congratulations!!!
Best wishes,
Andy Madaki
Outgoing—Curator
Abuja Hub

Several weeks before Thaine's visit, we applied for the Emerging Leaders Award program organized by Selfless4Africa and Abuja Global Shapers. We had put it out of our minds. It was just one of the numerous opportunities we had tried. Many had fallen through, so we didn't expect anything to come of this either. When this email came, we were out of options.

The national competition invited young people with novel ideas for community development to apply and try their chance to win a 1.1 million Naira grant to support their project. The email indicated that we qualified for the final stage, a presentation event in Abuja. They selected us as finalists from over two hundred applications across Nigeria.

On July 14th, 2018, Philip Dimka and I traveled to Abuja to make a case for our project. The other participants had professional-looking presentations with clean slides, beautiful photos, and detailed examples. We struggled to get our pitch ready on a single slide. Fortunately, we were the first to present, so we got it over with. Our lack of preparation was apparent. After four hours of different presentations, it was time to announce the winners.

The announcer stood up and began;

"We thank you for your commitment to your communities. We appreciate you for coming from different locations to partake in this pitch. We have listened to your presentations and have seen your slides. Our judges have made a decision. We have considered the sustainability of projects and the possible impact a project could have going forward. According to this criteria, the winner of the 2018 Emerging Leaders Award is Jenta Reads Community Initiative!"

We won! Now, we had 1.1 million Naira to bring to life the library we had always dreamed of.

Over the next six months, we worked together with Selfless4Africa and Abuja Global Shapers to utilize the funds to implement a library project in Jenta. We rented a three-room space and turned it into a library with a reading area, book section, and a computer room. As the project's implementation came to fruition, the values we had learned starting from scratch continued to shine. For instance, due to the absence of money, one crucial value we adopted was always to begin a project backward. We didn't assume there was money, for there was none, and since we assumed there was none, we would ask ourselves, "What part of this project can we do for free?"

With such frugal thinking, we've found that we could use the skills present in our Jenta Reads team members and defer spending money unless necessary. For instance, during the renovations, Peter Kurdor did the painting, Adams Yakubu tiled the floors, Supreme Gilbert designed and painted the signage, Clement Luka did the electrical work, Deshi Shedrach brought all the supplies, and all the other team members were present to help as needed—of course, for free. This was the actual service, the real volunteering.

This frugality was a marked departure from what we saw amongst other NGO networks in the country. Organizations often sought grants to execute projects and hired out all the required services, frequently leading to more professional results. However, it did not endear the workers to the ongoing project. The feeling generated when one builds a fence with one's own hands differs from when one out-sources the job to someone else. As the library took shape, we received more volunteers from the community, and it became common to hear community members ask what they could do to push it forward. Instead of seeing hired laborers working on the project, they saw their friends doing the work and naturally wanted to be a part of the fun. Now, they had a stake in the project and believed it belonged to them. They honestly said, "Jenta Reads is our library."

Theft

One vice that plagues Jenta is theft. As we stocked the library with books and computers, it became a serious concern that there would be a theft someday. These concerns became pronounced until we received a group of guests one day. They were young men from the jungle. We organized outreaches to the jungle every week and would invite them over to the library. They would come, and we would do Bible studies and share testimonies, challenges, and how we were growing. Then, we would pray together and share a meal.

Over time, the library became the place they visited whenever they were bored at home. The worst thing about the hood is that you have too much time on your hands. You must find creative ways to burn that time or get drawn into activities that would put you in trouble. The problem for a significant population was that they didn't have creative ways to spend that time. Now, they could spend their time at the library in a friendly environment devoted to learning. One fateful day, the major gang leaders from the jungle visited us. One spoke up and said, "We are aware that you've been concerned about the safety of this place. You are concerned that thieves will break in and steal stuff. We understand you. We are here to inform you that you need not worry about this. There will never be a theft here. We have passed a warning all around the jungle that no one should dare steal anything from the library. If anyone does, we will deal with that person ourselves. This library belongs to all of us. You guys worked hard to get it going to bless this community. We will not allow others to destroy your efforts. So, be at peace."

To this day, there has been no theft from the library, which is especially odd because, in the last ten years, theft within Jenta has gotten so bad that the police station within the community was closed down. The police were worried about the safety of their personnel. Ironically, it is likely that some of the same guys from the jungle perpetrated these robberies. They had come to trust us and become a part of the project. Building trust with recovering addicts who had multiple problems took months of visits and quiet listening. But the results were beginning to show. Most were more than willing to change their lives; they just didn't know what to do and didn't have the support network to change. God was using us to provide this support.

One night, during one of the frequent raids by gang boys in the community, I was unfortunate to be passing through the jungle as it was a shorter route to home. As the gang boys were constantly searching and seizing phones from community members, they confronted me. One guy pulled out a gun and shouted at me.

"Where is your phone? Where is your phone?"

I was about to pull it out when the other boy looked closely and said, "Ah. Senior man. Senior man. Nah. Don't touch this one. He is the senior man who helps us at the library. We cannot touch him." And so I passed. By this point, we had a solid rapport with the jungle guys and worked weekly to provide a path for redemption for many of them.

While I was sad for those who lost their property, this episode taught me that a new kind of spirit was sweeping Jenta. The change was happening, albeit at a slow pace. These culprits needed to develop a sense of responsibility not just towards me, but towards others in the community.

CHAPTER 17

THE RELENTLESS READER

The house of Zebulun Chinge Dodo shares a boundary with the library. He was present at the library commissioning in 2018 when he was just nine years old. Since then, he has become the most regular user of the library. He was present for almost every activity that involved his age group: hikes, film shows, debates, and Christmas funfairs. His introduction to books began with a set of The Chronicles of Narnia that Thaine had brought. Eventually, he read all the books in the library by C. S. Lewis, including the theological works. As time went on, books became Zebulun's best friends. He was no longer playing with his friends and was no longer interested in many other activities his peers participated in. His parents became worried about his reading and talked to me about it. His mother was afraid that he was reading too much. I told her there is no such thing, and more, would she prefer it if he was doing something dangerous like hanging out with boys in the jungle? Of course, she didn't want that. She was just worried that the reading would consume him. I told her it was nothing to worry about. Or so I thought.

One day, she called me to say she had a problem I had to solve.
"What happened?" I asked.

She answered, "It is Zebulun again."
"What did he do?" I asked.

That morning, Zebulun, about twelve years old by then, had told her he needed to talk and that she needed to be seated before he would speak to her. This is very unusual in an African home. The child never asks his parents to sit for a conversation. It is always the other way around. When she sat, he said, "Mummy, I have noticed how you have been treating us at home. Every time we offend you, you just beat us. For any mistake we make you spank us. You are also shouting at us and treating us like animals. You know, there is something called Human Rights. The United Nations says every human being has the right to live free and be free from any discrimination. This thing you are doing to us is against the rules of the UN. You could end up in the police station if we decide to report you. I have been thinking about this and I don't want to take any drastic action, that's why I am talking to you first."

The mother was too stunned to say anything. She didn't reply. Instead, she was calling me to report him. Zebulun had read a book related to the United Nations Human Rights Council from the library, and now he was applying the lessons he had learned. This book was just one of many that had made an impression on him. He influenced his other friends to begin reading, too, and these days, they compete for who will read the most books every year. Of course, they are blessed that Jenta Reads Community Library is there to provide all those books. My generation had none.

Zebulun went on to attend a highly-rated secondary school on the outskirts of Jos and became the Deputy Head Boy. I visited the school once for a graduation ceremony, and he rushed to greet me and introduce me to his friends. He told them this was the Lengdung he had said so much about. His uniform was neat, he had clean and well-trimmed hair, and his self-confidence was solid. He was the opposite of the average Jenta kid of my generation. He was the product of the new Jenta that has caught on since the founding of the Jenta Reads Community Library. He is confident about his abilities and does not worry about what he could be in the future. It is a sharp contrast to what I looked like in secondary school.

Here is a kid who has watched the movie and read the book *The Boy Who Harnessed the Wind*. Here is a kid who has new heroes in the Jenta Reads Team members, and here is a kid who has seen and heard, again and again, the message of hope at the library. What can stop him?

Giant Strides

The driving question at the library was always, "How can we serve this community?" The answers came up in the most interesting ways. Thaine's second visit was seven months later; this time, he brought his old friend, Eb Roell.

H. Eberhard Roell, an energetic and feisty German-American, was seventy-nine years old on his first visit to Jenta. According to Thaine, it was Eb who got him to visit Africa for the first time in 2013. Eb was a romantic adventurer who married Debbie, another romantic adventurer. Together, they decided to hitchhike around the world for their honeymoon, spending months in Africa. They fell in love with the continent and returned to Uganda as missionaries in the 1980s. Of course, it was perilous. They went through several coups d'etat. But in the midst of it all, they shared their lives and faith with the people they encountered. Eb is the sort of man in whom there is no pretense. His Christianity shines like a diamond. His story is chronicled in his autobiography, *Piercing The Night*.

Eb fit right in with the Jenta Reads team. This playful grandfather would tease and joke even as he taught us profound truths about life with Christ, such as when he would say things like, "In Him, we live, and move and have our dinner," a funny and yet accurate restatement of "In Him, we live, and move and have our being." In return, we teased him with a string of honorary titles such as "The Retired Most Right Reverend Professor Eb," or simply "The Professor." Of course, he was none of these, having only had a primary school education. This fact inspired us at Jenta Reads since it was through his reading and self-studies that Eb became a prolific social commentator, a missionary, and an author. If he could do that, so could we.

When Thaine and Eb returned for their second visit, Eb had brought some reading glasses of various strengths, which were gladly received by those with middle-aged eyesight. As a result, we began mulling over the idea of organizing a medical outreach. The pieces began to fit as we prayed about it and conversed with friends. Friends from the medical school at the university expressed a deep interest and offered their services for free. Doctors from Jos University Teaching Hospital, a prominent hospital in the city, offered to help if the outreach occurred on a weekend.

Within the Jenta Reads team, we had medical personnel such as Margaret Kingyong, a nurse, and Thaine's wife, Erika, a doctor. A plan crystallized, and in October 2019, we held the first medical outreach that provided basic health services to more than 1,200 residents of Jenta. We provided community members with glasses, toothbrushes, soaps, detergents, clothes, pads, and other essential healthcare items. It became an annual event. For many community members, it was the only time in the year that they got to see a doctor, partly due to a lack of resources and partly because the only government-sponsored clinic within the community rarely sees a doctor.

The health outreach fit easily into our vision for how Jenta Reads impacts the community. Only healthy people can read and learn effectively.

CHAPTER 18

Chess, Nathan, and the Lives We Are Changing

Three generations of Christians gathered when Thaine and Eb came in December 2018. Eb had been a mentor and discipler to Thaine. Thaine had been, and continues to be, a mentor and discipler to me. We talked about everything and shared so many life stories between us. Of course, I did most of the listening.

In our conversations, it came out that Eb was a chess expert.

"Hey Lengdung, do you play chess?" he asked.

"No. I don't know how to play."

"If you want to learn, I can teach you."

Eb had already come prepared with a chess board, so we began quick lessons. We moved to the library for more space, and more people joined our casual chess lessons. It was fun and a good way to spend time together. Eb couldn't miss any opportunity to teach biblical truths and wisdom for life, so we talked while we played chess. By the end of his visit, several people in Jenta had learned to play chess. He made a bet that on his next return if anyone could beat him at chess, the person would win a reward. All fingers were crossed.

One of the boys who had learned chess during this visit was twelve-year-old Nathan Abok. Nathan Abok was a student at ECWA Staff Secondary School. The following school session, after he had learned chess, the school announced the annual Inter-house competition. Students submitted their names and the fields in which they intended to compete. He submitted his name for the chess category to represent his house. While submitting his name, he had the typical Jenta-smacking conversation with his teacher: "What makes you think you can play chess? Chess is not a game for students from Jenta. It is an elite game for kids in better communities. We don't want you to lose for our house." Nathan insisted he was good at chess, so the teacher paired him up with another student for a trial. Nathan won the trial easily. Resigned, the teacher told him, "I am adding you as the representative of the house, but put it at the back of your mind that if you fail the house, I will deal with you."

The inter-house competition came, and Nathan did so well that he beat all the other houses and won the medal in chess for his house. They held a ceremony to crown each winner with a medal. He received his and didn't remove it for the next two days. On the way home, he made sure anyone who cared to listen heard his story about winning that medal. When he got home, he showed it to every family member. Finally, he brought it to the library to show us. He had heard of the low bar that was set for him and chose to rise above it. He said, "Now, I know I can do anything."

This was the very thing we had hoped and prayed for when we set out to start Jenta Reads. We wanted Jenta citizens to develop confidence in themselves and to see that they were not worthless. Nathan is currently enrolled in a nursing program.

Nathan was just one of many people who have been powerfully impacted at the library. The library has become a hub for the community. At the time of this writing, the library has 7,000 registered members, with about 930 books borrowed monthly. So many books

I had only dreamed of having for myself are now available to anyone who wishes to borrow them.

"I am Falling! I am Falling!"

Every year, we hold The Generational Debate, designed to help school children in Jenta confront the most important topics of their generation, such as climate change, Artificial Intelligence, poverty reduction, and the Sustainable Development Goals (SDGs). Debate winners receive financial rewards and other opportunities. For instance, in 2019, the debate winner was Shalom Private School, represented by three students: Faith, Jeremiah, and Simon, who went on to represent Jenta in another way.

After the debate, Jenta Reads was invited to join the Beyond The School Community Challenge, a program by the Mandela Washington Fellowship Association of Nigeria (MWFAAN) where students identify community problems and create solutions. Working with the winning school, the three students developed a solution for waste disposal. The solution was intriguing enough to be accepted into the Beyond The School Challenge and rated among the top twenty among three hundred projects. The next stage involved creating a video pitch, which secured their place among the top ten. The final stage required physical participation at an event in Abuja, the capital of Nigeria.

A Jenta Reads team member, Timothy Eneche, took Faith, Jeremiah, and Simon to Abuja to participate. They entered an elevator at the hotel, which began moving upward. Faith held on to Timothy, screaming, "I am falling! I am falling! It is moving! It is moving! It will throw me down!"

It was her first time entering an elevator or staying in a hotel. Traveling to Abuja was the first time she had ever left home. In fact, these were first-time experiences for all three participants. They went on to perform well, taking third place, and they returned home with cash prizes. For the rest of the year, they could not stop talking about their adventures. The experience had enlarged their world.

Faith came to the library one day after the group returned home and said, "Sir, I have a question. I've always thought that to be a journalist was beyond my place, but I saw a woman in Abuja who said she was a journalist. I want to be a journalist. Do you think I can do it?"

"Of course you can. You can be anything you set your heart to be."

Faith, who formerly believed herself to be a nobody from nowhere-Jenta, is currently studying journalism at the University of Jos.

Saving Lives

The library provided a space for dreaming and a safe space for healing. In 2022, Esther Akus walked to the library to browse the books. We chit-chatted a bit about how she was doing and how life was treating her, and she explained that she was doing okay. I asked again if she was sure she was okay. She said she was, except that she had been robbed a few days earlier. She had gone for morning exercise when gang boys stopped her on the road and robbed her of her phone. I expressed my condolences to her and asked if it was just the phone they had taken from her. She replied in the affirmative. We talked a bit more before she left the library. I don't know why I persisted in asking her. Sometimes, God leads you to do things you have no explanation for.

Later that day, I received a text message from her. It said, "Lengdung, hope you are doing well. That time in the morning, you asked if the phone was the only thing that was taken from me. I told you yes, but that's not the whole story. It wasn't the only thing. I was also raped. I couldn't tell you there because there were people. And I haven't told anyone except you because no one has asked. My family has been blaming me for going to exercise with my phone. I cannot bear to see their reaction if I told them I was also raped." I expressed sympathy and asked if she wanted to meet and talk. She said yes. We met, and she told me the whole story.

She was out exercising that morning when the gang boys stopped her at the junction. They stopped a few other people, too. After they took her phone, the gang leader said she was too beautiful for him to let her go just like that, and he asked the boys to "take her down." They took her to drainage ditch on the roadside. Two boys held her while he forced his way with her; when he was done and left, the other boys also did the same.

She was too broken to say anything to anyone. She was ashamed. Ours is a deeply patriarchal society that still holds theories such that it is always the women who, by the way they dress, provoke the men to rape them. She lived in this painful silence for two days until I met her. When Esther visited the library, she came because she didn't know where else to go and had not come to borrow any books. She was just wandering the community because of her restlessness. At that time, Esther was thinking of suicide. She wanted to end it all. How could she live with it? What if she "took in," and became pregnant? No one would believe that she had been raped. What would people say of her? She couldn't take it. She couldn't live with this. She wanted everything to be over. Of course, she was angry with the world and with God.

As I listened to her, I tried to assure her she could get through this—however, some things needed to be done. First, we needed to get to the hospital to get some tests. Second, she needed to speak to a professional or an adult who could help her. I gave her some money, and she took some tests at the hospital. The one thing that preoccupied her mind was that she did not want to be pregnant. She said if the test returned positive, she would not return home; she would kill herself. The doctors said the pregnancy results could not be determined until some time had passed. In my mind, I said, "Praise God, that was enough time to pray and walk with her to change her mind."

I asked her if she was open to talking to someone else. I told her I would make sure it was private and that the person would be someone she could trust, never to reveal her secret. She agreed. That someone turned out to be Meredith DeVoe. We met at their home, and Bob was there, too.

While there, Esther broke down completely. She told the story again with tears in her eyes and expressed all her painful emotions. Meredith and Bob were so helpful; they provided good listening ears and counsel and earned her trust. From then on, the conversation continued. Gradually, she dropped the idea of killing herself. Now, she was asking the question of whether to abort the baby or to keep the pregnancy. Meredith, Bob, and I assured her that we would support and provide for her, whatever decision she made. After some weeks, we found out she hadn't become pregnant. It was a massive sigh of relief for all.

For Esther, the healing was still ongoing. We met consistently at least once every two weeks for a whole year. We walked with her through her emotions, anger, pain, and regret. The horrific event damaged her self-esteem, her trust in people, and her worldview. Rebuilding all of that was like learning to be human again. It was a testament to her resilience that she grew beyond this within a year. However, if the Jenta Reads Community Library had not been present, it is hard to imagine that she would have gotten past thinking about suicide. It is hard to imagine that she would have had the support to move on from this tragic incident.

It was because of needs like this that Jenta Reads came to be. It was our dream to provide a safe space in a community with many dangers.

Many women have found the same kind of help through Jenta Reads: women with abusive husbands, girls living with abusive relatives, single mothers struggling with raising children and living in a society that constantly judges them. They come to the library regularly as the one place where they can sit and have someone listen to them, and oftentimes, they get material support to help them cope.

Sometimes, all a person needs is someone willing to listen. Jenta Reads exists to listen to a community.

Outreach to women has been a central pillar of Jenta Reads. Women in the Jenta Reads Team have been at the forefront of ensuring that the particularities of the women's world are considered and adequately cared for. One month, Longdi Sylvanus, Peace Agowa, Manna Mamfat, and the other women on the team organized a menstrual hygiene program. They taught young girls to understand their bodies, build confidence, and use hygiene packs properly. Cultural barriers make conversations about puberty very difficult. During the first session, the presence of some male Jenta Reads team members made the atmosphere uncomfortable. When Peace realized this, she turned to Philip and said, "Alright, Phil. Gather up your men. All of you, leave here. This is a women's gathering." That day opened a new chapter for many girls. They opened up about their experiences in ways that no one imagined. They discussed women's issues ranging from puberty to men's advances to family problems and educational pursuits. The session's overwhelming success led to it becoming a regular event held at least once a month. At the end of the session, girls received pads; for many, it was the first pad they ever received. Now, a pad container in the library allows girls to help themselves discreetly whenever needed.

Abdul

As Jenta Reads progressed, one of those who came around to support us was Abdul my roommate and friend from ANA. My arguments with Abdul deepened our friendship. Abdul graduated one year after me from All Nations Academy. Our friendship continued. We shared books between us. Abdul leaned towards community development in his community, even as I leaned towards community development in mine. We shared ideas, encouraged each other, and supported each other. Abdul became one of the few Muslims who visited Jenta without fear years after the crisis. He was confident I would protect him.

He also introduced me to his circle, mostly Muslims. Within that circle, I met another Abdul. His full name was Abdulrasheed Doma. This Abdul was also a book lover. He was also interested in community development. One day, Abdul Doma sent me a message saying he wanted to volunteer with Jenta Reads and make his life useful to humanity. Since then, he has been a part of Jenta Reads, contributing to developing Jenta with his time, energy, and resources. I have visited Abdul's hometown of Kanam, a predominantly Muslim community, to deliver a speech at a program he organized for the town's students.

One generation ago, my forebears were chasing the likes of Abdul and his people, and his people were also chasing my people. Now, we are working together to make Jenta a better place. Our religious differences have not torn us apart. We are understanding each other's beliefs one day at a time. The presence of Abdul in the Jenta Reads Team summarizes our approach to the future we envision for Jenta, Plateau State, and Nigeria as a whole: a place where religious differences, tribal differences, and regional differences do not lead to bloodshed but understanding and diversity. Diversity is beautiful.

Spreading Inspiration

In 2020, Nenkinan Nehemiah Deshi invited me to deliver a TEDx Talk at TEDx UniJos. In it, I shared the story of Jenta Reads, beginning by describing my upbringing and the challenges Jenta faced; after that, I explained how we were trying to change the narrative through Jenta Reads. It was a speech that ended with a standing ovation from the audience. I received many messages that day from young people saying they were inspired by what we were doing. Nenkinan Deshi teamed up with Kangyang Hyelni to start a community library effort in Jebbu Miango to provide reading materials to a community that has been a victim of violent attacks in Plateau State, Nigeria. They've named their efforts Jebbu Miango Reads. Other libraries within Jos have also sprouted up. Tudun Wada Reads, Angwan Rukuba Reads, and Noel Bewarang Memorial Library. These efforts are solving their community problems in unique ways using the tools of education. They were all inspired by Jenta Reads, but these are also grassroots efforts driven by people who live in the communities and understand their problems better than anyone from the outside would understand. We have supported them in whatever ways we could, but we are not the major drivers of these initiatives.

Change cannot begin from the outside. Change must start from within. Young people must believe they can change their destiny and rise to the occasion. All we can do is support them.

Jenta Kid

These days, I am invited to deliver speeches at prestigious events throughout Nigeria. Each time I introduce myself and say I am from Jenta, I get responses like "Really? That's unbelievable. You don't look like someone from there. You are too refined to be from that slum."

But it's true. I am a product of Jenta. I was fortunate to be set in motion by my parents when they sent me to a school eighty kilometer from Jenta. I was gifted with great friendships with Peter Emmanuel, Anita Clarkson, and Thaine Norris. I was happy to have encountered books early in life. And I was blessed to have experienced the mercy of God.

"An object will remain in a state of rest or uniform motion unless an external force acts upon it." I experienced many different external forces that set me on a different path. I could have been a spoiled soup, for indeed, I was for many years, but today many know me as Lengdung, "the one who thinks deeply." I hope to live up to it.

Although this story is a story of motion, a movement away from Jenta, away from its forces and habits, I have gone full circle. Ever since I saw the possibility of another world, the rest of my life has moved *toward* Jenta. Jenta and its problems are the new focus of my life. Our lives, actually. I had the privilege of having a different path than the typical Jenta kid would have, my mission is to ensure many more kids get the same opportunity. It is why we started Jenta Reads. It is why I wrote this book. It is why I woke up this morning. It is why I will wake up tomorrow. And it is why I will wake up every other day until God calls me home. I am a Jenta boy, I will always be.

FOR THE LOVE OF BOOKS

Once you fall in love with books, you can't fall out of love again. Perhaps life can get so busy that you struggle to find time, but the love for those beautiful things can never be destroyed. Since 2016, I have read 80-100 books almost every year. I share the reviews with my social media community, especially on Facebook, which has attracted 450,000 people as of this writing.

I have distributed books through giveaways to my audience outside Plateau State, mainly young people inspired by my social media posts promoting reading. I knew that reading had changed my life, and I know it could change theirs.

On October 13th, 2021, I received a phone call.

"Hello. Am I speaking to Lengdung Tungchamma?"

"Hi. This is Lengdung. Who is on the line?"

"My name is Fabian George. I am the director of Books Focus, an international NGO that distributes books to Africa. I am visiting Nigeria to expand our work, to give more books to young people, and to help establish some libraries. You were highly recommended as one of those who have been involved in book distribution. Your expertise could be of great help in this. I believe you understand the importance of reading, and how it can change people's lives. We are excited to change people's lives. Is this something you are interested in?"

"Ah. Amazing. Thank you so much for reaching out. I am honored. Yes, books have transformed me, and I am confident they will transform others too. I will be glad to be of any help in this. Count me in."

"Awesome. So, there is one challenge though, I am in the country for only a few days. I am currently headed to Jos from Abuja. We have to meet tomorrow for this to happen."

"Whew. Sorry. That will be a hard one. I am not available tomorrow."

"My flight leaves the country tomorrow. My best shot at meeting you is before I return to catch up with the flight. If we can't work this around, it would be impossible to proceed. I've already heard a lot about you, and I am confident that all we need to do is talk over a few things and sign the papers. After that, we can continue the conversation online."

"I am quite sorry, I can't make it tomorrow. It will be a full day for me as it is my wedding."

"Ah. Really? Congratulations. It seems we can't meet then. Hmmmmmmmm... (pause) The opportunity has to pass by. (pause) Is there no opportunity for a brief meeting before the wedding? It could be really brief. I just need to see, take a photo or two, and sign papers. That will be it. I will really appreciate this."

"Hmmmmm... Okay. Let's see. This is very important to me, too. Do you think we can meet very early in the morning?"

At that point, there was loud laughter from the other side of the phone. Unknown to me, I was on a call with a radio station. My friend, Rejoice Shammah, wanted to wish me a happy married life, so she played a prank on me. She devised this scheme with the confidence that she knew I would never turn down the opportunity to distribute books, even on my wedding day. My love for books had been exposed on a radio program broadcast live to millions of people in Plateau State.

On October 14th, 2021, Senfat Machief and I were joined together at our local church. Some months prior, the two of us sat at the library talking about our shared memories when I asked her, "Will you let me take care of you?" Thus began the courtship that led to our marriage. She makes marriage easy.

On the wedding day, as part of the ceremony, Reverend Bob DeVoe prayed for us. In one of those prayers, he said, "We pray for more books in this family." God has answered this prayer for me, my wife, and Jenta Reads.

Together with Thaine, we have established Walking Together Press, a non-profit publishing company supporting African libraries. The company motto is, "We sell books so that we can give books away." Our first project to bring books to places with no books is the *Jenta Reads Essential Library,* which comprises one hundred of the most impactful books we've read. We are distributing these hundred-volume collections to schools and communities as starter libraries. I did not have access to anywhere near one hundred books when my reading journey began, so we hope that this collection can set people on a faster journey to discover new worlds.

During Thaine's visits, our book discussions would naturally evolve into conversations about the value of reading. We'd visit schools to encourage and inspire the students to explore the world of books, discovering the treasures and insights that await them within. However, these schools had no libraries or books. Our words could have fallen on fertile ground, but there was no environment to nourish growth. With the Jenta Reads Essential Library, we go beyond mere inspiration to providing the materials.

We can make Jenta Reads available to those outside Jenta.

There is a kid like me somewhere out there who will pick up The Chronicles of Narnia like I did. Who knows what might result? I can't wait to hear those stories.

Walking Together Press is a non-profit publishing company devoted to supporting grassroots libraries in Africa through global book sales and through providing free library editions.

To read our story, to see our catalog, and to learn more about how you can help us in our mission, visit our website at:

walkingtogether.press